God's Holy Hill

God's Holy Hill

A History of Christianity
in Cuddesdon

Mark D. Chapman

THE WYCHWOOD PRESS

For John Paxton

Our books may be ordered from bookshops or (post free) from
Jon Carpenter Publishing, Alder House, Market Street, Charlbury, OX7 3PH
01608 811969

e-mail: wychwood@joncarpenter.co.uk

Credit card orders should be phoned or faxed to 01689 870437 or 01608 811969

Please send for our free catalogue

First published in 2004 by
The Wychwood Press
an imprint of Jon Carpenter Publishing
Alder House, Market Street, Charlbury, Oxfordshire OX7 3PH

ISBN 1 902279 20 4

Printed in England by Antony Rowe Ltd., Eastbourne

Contents

Abbreviations

BOD: Bodleian Library, Oxford

CC: C.F. Slade and Gabrielle Lambrick (eds.), *Two Cartularies of Abingdon Abbey*, vol 2: Chatsworth Cartulary, Oxford: Oxford Historical Society, 1990

CMA: Joseph Stevenson, *Chronicon Monasterii de Abingdon*, Rolls Series: vol. 1, *From the Foundation of the Monastery Until the Norman Conquest*; vol. 2, *From the Conquest until the accession of Richard I*, London: Longman, 1858

COS: Oxfordshire County Council Centre for Oxfordshire Studies

EPNS: English Place Names Society

HEA: John Hudson (ed.), *Historia Ecclesie Abbendonensis: The History of the Church in Abingdon*, Oxford: Clarendon Press, vol. 2, 2002

LC: C.F. Slade and Gabrielle Lambrick (eds.), *Two Cartularies of Abingdon Abbey*, vol. 1: Lyell Cartulary

LRS: Lincolnshire Record Society

MB: All Saints' Cuddesdon Parish Church PCC Minute Book, from 1919

MC: Mark D. Chapman, photographs by author

OHS: Oxford Historical Society

ORS: Oxfordshire Record Society

RCC: Ripon College Cuddesdon Archives

SFC: S.R. Wigram (ed.), *The Cartulary of the Monastery of St. Frideswide at Oxford*, Oxford: Oxford Historical Society, 28, 1895 (vol. i) & 31, 1896 (vol. ii)

VCH: *The Victoria History of the County of Oxford*, London: Archibald Constable; Oxford: Oxford University Press for the University of London Institute of Historical Research, from 1907.

VCH, i, vol. 1, L.F. Salzman (ed.), *Natural history, Early Man, Romano-British & Anglo-Saxon remains, Domesday survey, Political History, Schools*, 1939

VCH, ii, vol. 2, William Page (ed.), *Ecclesiastical History, Religious Houses, Social and Economic History, Industries, Ancient Earthworks, Sport*, 1907

VCH, v, vol. 5, Mary D. Lobel (ed.), *Bullingdon Hundred*, 1959

List of Illustrations

Preface

This book began as a revision of a folded A4 sheet that used to be placed at the back of the Church in Cuddesdon. It rather took over my spare moments when I should have been devoting my energies to my academic interests in modern theology and to helping run a theological college. But in the end it has emerged and I am especially pleased that Jon Carpenter has been so ready to accept it for publication. Photographs from the Centre for Oxfordshire Studies are reproduced with permission and are © Oxfordshire County Council Photographic Archive. Pictures from the Bodleian library are reproduced with permission. I am grateful to Dr R. G. Newhouse for the photograph of Edward Elton, his great grandfather, and Edward King. I am also grateful to the Principal of Ripon College Cuddesdon for permission to reproduce photographs from the extensive College archives so splendidly kept by John Davies.

Many people have helped me in writing this book and in correcting my many errors. In particular the Revd Jason St John Nicolle read through the entire text and helped me improve it at many points. He also suggested many bibliographical resources in medieval history. I am also extremely grateful to Professor Diarmaid MacCulloch of St Cross College, Oxford for reading through the entire text with extraordinary efficiency and also for contributing his lively foreword. Many parishioners and clergy helped correct my impressions of twentieth century history – Cyril Sellar was the source of many anecdotes, only some of which could find their way into the book. Mrs Mary Palmer let me look round Dove House and Gilbert Howes showed me evidence of the Manor House. There were also many other people in Cuddesdon, most especially my wife, Linda Collins, who helped in many ways through their conversations and through supporting me in a project that seemed to have no end. I am also grateful to the loyal congregation of All Saints' Church for indulging me in my many historical sermons over the past few years. One name stands out in particular: John Paxton, who retired as Churchwarden in 2004, has been a great supporter of the church and village. His unflappable and down to earth manner combined with great pastoral sensitivity and wit are what every church needs. It is to him that this book is affectionately dedicated.

Foreword

It is a pleasure and a privilege to introduce this excellent survey of one English village's religious life over more than a thousand years. It splendidly places a single community in a wider context, transcending deficiencies in the surviving original local evidence, which before the nineteenth century is unusually scarce. Through a patchwork of thousands of such parish stories, we can understand the greater story which has extended beyond the Church and Kingdom of England, to embrace a worldwide Christian identity called Anglicanism.

As I remember from my own happy year at Ripon College Cuddesdon, one of the pleasures of the Cuddesdon experience is the contradictory nature of the place: by dint of being untypical, it manages to seem a snapshot of everyone's image of the typical English village, and this pleasing paradox has been built into a history full of oddity. Archaeological discoveries make it likely that still lurking in the soil is further evidence of Cuddesdon's special role in Anglo-Saxon royal life. Later, the village was blessed by the monks of Abingdon with a church whose unusual stateliness suggests that it may have been intended as something more than simply a place for the parish's worship. Later still, the village became linked to the fortunes of one of the Church of England's most idiosyncratic (and idiosyncratically-endowed) dioceses, through an episcopal palace whose repeated destruction by fire might inspire in Lady Bracknell unsympathetic remarks about carelessness, and via constitutional arrangements which linked the parish's pastoral care to some of the most distinguished clergy in the Church of England. Among these clergy, Bishop Wilberforce masterminded the foundation of the College: its facade by that inspired Victorian architect George Edmund Street was intended primarily to be viewed from the Bishop's front windows, and the design can still only fully be appreciated by taking up that viewpoint, from the ground where the lost Palace once stood. As a living community, the College remains one of the witnesses in Anglicanism to a religious tradition of calm sanity and open-mindedness – a very necessary witness in today's Church, where many appear not to prize such qualities. I hope that the religious tradition of this delightful place will long be nurtured in the fruitful if tangled relationship between a small village and the large ecclesiastical cuckoo in its nest.

DIARMAID MacCULLOCH
Professor of the History of the Church, Oxford University
St. Cross College, Oxford: Epiphany 2004.

Chapter One

Cuddesdon Before the Norman Conquest

Introduction

There was once a village legend that Cuddesdon meant 'God's Hill'. While this is undoubtedly purely fanciful, it nevertheless conveys something of the atmosphere of a village in which the presence of the Church has been more strongly felt than perhaps anywhere else in England.[1] And it is probably also true that, for good or ill, the village of Cuddesdon with its Bishop's Palace and Theological College, has left its own indelible mark on the Church of England. It is a village whose history has been inextricably bound up with abbots, bishops and clergy for well over a thousand years. It consequently comes as something of a surprise to learn that nobody has ever written a full-scale history of Christianity in Cuddesdon.[2] An important source of revenue for the monks of Abingdon before the dissolution of the monasteries, Cuddesdon, which perches on an outcrop of oolitic limestone, provided a splendid location to display monastic wealth and power to the surrounding low-lying valleys. After the dissolution of the monasteries and the foundation of the diocese of Oxford the village was to be the home of the Bishops of Oxford for much of the time from the 1630s to the 1970s, and from 1854 it has housed a Theological College (now called Ripon College Cuddesdon) which has educated many thousands of clergy in the Church of England and in the wider Anglican Communion. Memories of Cuddesdon and its parish church continue to inspire clergy throughout the world.

To write a history of Christianity in Cuddesdon is thus not simply to chronicle the development of a majestic and beautiful building served by a series of now forgotten clergy. Instead, almost the whole history of Christianity in England has been expressed in microcosm in one small Oxfordshire village. As many of the events in the book reveal, Cuddesdon played a bit part in many of the great events in the history of the English church and state. At the same time, however, the history of Christianity in Cuddesdon is the history of Christians, some famous, others less so, who in their different ways have shaped the life of the village, and often the life of the church and the world outside.

Cuddesdon in Roman and Anglo-Saxon times: from Paganism to Christianity

It is not clear precisely when Christianity first made its appearance in Cuddesdon – indeed it is quite impossible to know when human beings first settled in the area of the ancient parish.[3] The earliest traces of civilisation which have been found are those of an isolated but significant Roman villa which was discovered in 1845 on what is now called Castle Hill about half way between Cuddesdon and Wheatley: Cuddesdon was not far from the Dorchester to Alchester (near Bicester) road, which ran past the present-day car works and along the edge of Horspath. James Henry Parker, the Oxford antiquarian and afterwards curator of the Ashmolean, Dr William Bromet, the antiquarian, and Mr Sanders, the schoolmaster at the National School at Wheatley, undertook an excavation of what was reported as a 'luxurious mansion'[4] which contained a substantial hypocaust. Later the Bishop of Oxford[5] organised a further excavation with permission from the owner, T. Grove of Shaftesbury, calling on the services of Dr William Buckland (Dean of Westminster from 1845-56) and Parker. They discovered another portion of the villa 116 feet to the north, which indicated a very substantial dwelling. This included a large cistern or 'boiler', and the remains of a bathhouse with a frigidarium of 8ft x 4ft and a caldarium of 14ft x 12ft. Several coins were also found dating from the reigns of Maximianus (292-311) to Gratianus (375-383). Glass was discovered similar to that found earlier at Holton: several of the fragments were apparently arranged by Sanders in the School House in Wheatley, and later deposited in the Ashmolean Museum in Oxford. Although the report is fairly comprehensive, the heritage industry of those days was rather less developed, and even though for some years the site was protected by a shed,[6] this was later taken away which means that the exact location has now been lost; all that was noted is that it was three furlongs from the River Thame and near the footpath to Wheatley over Castle Hill. By 1872 it was reported every stone of the villa had disappeared.[7]

In 1916 it was somewhat cursorily reported that 'a discovery of Roman remains of very considerable interest has been made among the shrubberies in the northern part of the Bishop's grounds at Cuddesdon, indicating a large villa of about AD 300'. This included a 'remarkable underground passage, bending in a most unusual form, and lined and roofed with large stone slabs'.[8]

Unfortunately the find was not well documented, and further enquiries were made in 1921 in preparation for a second excavation. A letter from E. T. Leeds to Dr A. W. Coombs[9] notes that 'from enquiries made of Gardener ... the last excavations were made in 1916 by Butler [? – the writing is unclear] who has now left the neighbourhood. The site appears to be 30 yards long.' Leeds lists the find as including 'tiles, iron, debris, a bronze fibula' and various other artefacts. It was perhaps near to the stonepit in Dove House Farm, where a hypocaust and various fragments of South Gaulish pottery as well as eight coins were unearthed. There were no signs of tessellated floors. Two brooches, which are now in the Ashmolean Museum, indicate a date between the third and fourth centuries.[10] Davies adds that the curate at the time, who had apparently helped with the excavations, noted piping from the heating. He also claimed that a further simple house was found in 1921 built on earlier foundations, although there is no further corroboration for this. He might have been confused by the Oxford University Archaeological Society's investigation of the site in 1921 under Dudley Buxton. In a 'little garden' to the north of the palace, where many previous finds had been made, 'fragmentary foundations' of the house were discovered, but it was impossible to follow the line of the house due to trees. Nevertheless a 'good deal of pottery of all kinds' was found, including Samian and locally-made ware. Nothing was discovered earlier than the second century.[11] There is thus evidence of settlement in and around Cuddesdon in the late period of Roman occupation. It is obviously quite feasible that the first Christians might have come to this area in those early years.

In the couple of centuries that followed the end of the Roman occupation, however, there is a complete absence of any evidence of human settlement in Cuddesdon. Nevertheless, from widespread archaeological evidence elsewhere, it is clear that the Upper Thames Valley soon became an important centre of early Saxon settlement, and it may well be that some of the outlying hills near the valleys of its tributaries were cultivated and consequently became home to small scattered settlements. At the time, however, such settlements were seldom fixed, as farmers moved from one pasture to the next when it had been farmed out.[12]

There is evidence of a Saxon presence near the village in the earliest period of settlement in the late sixth century. In 1882 Henry Gale's workers were clearing the large field on Castle Hill of large stones which prevented the use of the steam plough.[13] About half a mile from the site of the Roman villa, they made a chance find of a skeleton. This revealed a large burial site: a further 57 graves were later unearthed.[14] The early part of the dig was haphazard and poorly documented, and by the time the Ashmolean Museum became

Above 1.1. 1883 Excavation. Henry Taunt (COS)
Below 1.2. Skeletons from 1883 Excavation. Henry Taunt (COS)

involved on 29 January 1883, twenty four graves had already been discovered with many grave goods including two shield bosses, three spear heads, and an ivory comb. The later finds were better documented: there were many funerary objects, only one of which, a Celtic pin, was of particular importance. Most of the objects were modest, which indicates a comparatively poor community.[15] Leeds notes that the date of the graves would probably be after 571 when the area became relatively peaceful. Also significant is the fact that one of the skeletons was found in a prone position, which might indicate a connection with the other (probably later) Saxon cemetery found forty years earlier in the Bishop's wood. The Castle Hill cemetery shows no evidence of Christianity or of cremation.

A chance find was made during the enlargement of the Bishop's Palace by Samuel Wilberforce in 1847. Despite poor documentation this has proved to be an important source of information about Anglo-Saxon England. In constructing a new driveway to the Palace for the new bishop, workmen unearthed a number of human bones.[16] It was reported in the *Archaeological Journal* later in the same year that 'several human skeletons' were found 'at a depth of between two and three feet from the surface. On further examination it became clear that the skeletons were arranged in a circle, the heads outwards, lying on their faces with their legs crossed. They were in a state of high preservation.' Near them were found 'several highly curious and interesting objects': two 'very decayed' swords, two squat blue glass bowls, one of 3 inches high and 5⅞ inches diameter and the other smaller, a bronze bucket, '9 inches high and much worn', a fragment of gilt bronze set with garnets (which has been interpreted as a bird's head and may have been an ornamental plaque for a shield or even a musical instrument), and a late medieval sealing ring with the word Pax.[17] This fascinating collection of ancient artefacts was exhibited by the Bishop to the Society of Antiquaries in November 1852, and coloured plates of the bucket and the glass vessels were published by J. Y. Akerman in 1855.[18]

It now seems extraordinary that at some stage after this date all the objects were lost, although one of the bowls was rediscovered by Jocelyn Morris, curator of Warwick Museum, in 1971. It was in the possession of Mrs Boughton-Leigh of Newbold-upon-Avon near Rugby, and was reportedly being used as a flower vase filled with primroses. It is now in the care of the Ashmolean Museum.[19] There is no account of how this bowl came into the possession of the family. Although initially the bowls were thought to be medieval, primarily because the find also contained medieval artefacts, later archaeologists have authenticated the Anglo-Saxon origin of the bowls. They may well have been of Kentish manufacture, which perhaps points to a date immediately following 600 when such glassware was known to have been manufactured there; the missing bowl was squat with a collared neck with three thick applied glass trails pinched to form two rows of lozenge shaped cells and is similar to one found in the second ship burial at Sutton Hoo.[20]

The bucket, which showed evidence of having been repaired before the

1.3. The Cuddesdon Bowls or Vases from J. Y. Akerman, *Remains of Pagan Saxondom*, Plate VI, pp. 11-12.

burial, is unique in Europe. It was originally thought to have been of Anglo-Saxon manufacture,[21] but it seems more likely to have originated in Coptic Egypt. Martin Conway wrote that the 'incomplete form postulates a stand into which the base should fit. An example of the complete utensil is no. 9051 in Cairo Museum. The English example is unique in this country. The Cairo

1.4. The Cuddesdon Bucket from J. Y. Akerman, *Remains of Pagan Saxondom*, Plate XIII, pp. 25-6.

example belongs to a series clearly Coptic. It follows that the Cuddesdon bucket is a Coptic import into England.'[22] Although this is obviously conjectural, it would again help date the grave to the early seventh century when such luxury goods were beginning to appear in England. In the initial report there was some conjecture that the bucket, which 'resembles in form to the *situla* or holy-water stoup',[23] showed evidence of Christianity, a theory which was repeated in 1931 by W. J. Andrew and R. A. Smith.[24] However, this seems co-incidental: there are few Christian burials with such lavish grave goods. Importantly, the quality of the objects reveals that whoever it was that was buried in Cuddesdon was wealthy and may well have been associated with the political power that was beginning to emerge in the Upper Thames Valley in the early seventh century.[25] This means that the most likely date for the burial is during the reign of Aethelbert after Caewlin's death in 593 and before Aethelbert's own death in 616.[26]

Although it was impossible to be certain of the precise location of the 1847 site, further excavations by Tania Dickinson in 1970 revealed at least four more bodies: an adult male and adult female, another female of about 20 years of age, and a child aged between about eight and puberty. She also found a bronze label tag. Her work has shown the Cuddesdon find to be of national significance, and quite different from the normal pattern of Anglo-Saxon burials: radial burials are rare, but uniform prone burial is unique.[27] It is likely, although far from certain, that the burial at Cuddesdon occurred in a barrow where a number of skeletons were placed around a central figure. It is important to note, however, that no central skeleton was ever found, which might indicate a cremation.[28] Most interesting about the Cuddesdon burial, however, is the prone position and the crossed legs which may possibly indicate that they were bound together. This, as Dickinson points out, seems 'to suggest something more sinister than natural death'.[29] It is quite possible (although again far from certain) that these skeletons were the unfortunate victims of a sacrifice associated with the burial of the central figure. Although such sacrifice was not reported in Britain by the early missionaries, it was known in the Germanic world. Dickinson concludes that the best if gruesome explanation of the find would seem to be a human sacrifice which occurred at the time of the burial of the wealthy man.

The quality of the funerary objects indicates that the site at Cuddesdon may well have been a 'princely' burial, although any evidence for royal activity in the Cuddesdon area in the early seventh century is purely circumstantial. Not long after the burial, however, the old Roman settlement at Dorchester-on-Thames was chosen as the location of the see of the first bishop of the West Saxons, St Birinus. This choice of an old Roman town means that it may well have been the site of royal occupation. Similarly, military activity is known to have taken place in the area, and it soon became the centre of Mercian incursions in their efforts to control the Thames. However, this still makes the choice of Cuddesdon itself as a princely burial site difficult to explain, since it was undoubtedly not a royal centre like Dorchester or Benson. In her attempt to explain the location, Dickinson notes the earlier Saxon find from Wheatley which indicates a Saxon settlement with some connection with the working of precious metals.[30] The remainder of the Cuddesdon estate was probably wooded or waste-land. This would mean that it would have been suitably remote for the burial, especially one accompanied by human sacrifice. It is even feasible that the tenth-century royal estate which was granted by Edwig (or Edwy) to his thegn, Aelfere, in the year 956 is in fact of a much earlier origin than the charter, and it might even have been a royal possession at the time of the burial. If this is the case then this might explain the choice of Cuddesdon.[31]

It is also possible that the place name of Cuddesdon itself provides evidence for this princely connection. In the 956 Charter the name is given as '*Cuthenes dune*', (which probably means 'hill of Cuthwines')[32] which uses the personal form Cuthen in its genitive inflected form.[33] The same name is also used with the suffix *hlaew* (meaning barrow mound) at Cutteslowe,[34] which was possibly the burial place of Cutha who was killed at Fethanleag (Stoke Lyne) in 584. Another *cudan hlaewe* is found in the charter boundary for Cuxham, and the same Cutha might possibly have given his name to a field called 'Cuddington' near Watlington.[35] The same person might also lie behind the name of Cuddington just over the border in Buckinghamshire. It is impossible to know, however, whether one man gave his name to a number of settlements, or whether there were a number of men after whom the different settlements were named. The *cuth*- prefix was common in the West Saxon dynasty from about 550 to 680.[36] Nevertheless, Dickinson suggests, the association of the different Wessex place names with one another 'remains something of a probability, and the occurrence of one of them at the site of a probable "princely" burial may be more than a co-incidence'.[37]

In her survey of Anglo-Saxon archaeology in Oxfordshire, Sonia Hawkes is rather less cautious. She suggests that the dead man 'might well have been' the overlord, Cuthwine (or Cutha), the brother of Ceawlin (d. 593), a great and well-attested kingly war-leader of the late sixth century, from whom the seventh century kings of the west Saxons were descended.[38] Cuthwine is mentioned in the Anglo-Saxon Chronicle in association with Ceawlin, fighting against Britons and slaying three kings at Dyrham in 577, and capturing three cities, Gloucester, Cirencester and Bath.[39] He may be the same person as Cuthwulf who fought the Battle of Biedcanford in 571. Given that there was much British opposition to Ceawlin's rule of the West Saxons, this would have made Cuthwine a major *sub-regulus* in the campaigns against the British: the granting of an estate at Cuddesdon on a hill at the edge of the West Saxon territory facing the Chilterns to the king's brother would certainly have made strategic sense.[40] All this is obviously speculative, but it seems not unreasonable to suppose that the estate was in the hands of the princely families from the very beginnings of Saxon rule, and that one of those princes, perhaps Cuthwine himself, was laid to rest in the grounds of the Bishop's Palace with rituals possibly involving human sacrifice. While there must be some doubt about whether the graves show evidence of human sacrifice, what is almost certain is that they are pre-Christian, since after the conversion of the West Saxons there was a rapid decline in the placing of funerary ornaments in graves.

The Coming of Christianity

Paganism was not to last much longer. Although it is impossible to know when Christianity was first preached in Cuddesdon, or even if there was a permanent settlement in Cuddesdon in these times, it is clear that Christianity came to the Upper Thames valley forty years or so after Ceawlin's death in 593. During the rule of Cynegils, who reigned from 611-43, St Birinus was sent by Pope Honorius as a missionary to England in about 634. Very little is known of Birinus' life before his ordination by Asterius, archbishop of Milan, although he may have been a native of Genoa, receiving his education at the monastery of Bobbio.[41] By the time Birinus arrived in Britain, Christianity had already been established in Northumbria, Lindsey, East Anglia and Kent (following Augustine's mission of 597), often building on pre-existing foundations and the work of the Irish missionaries. Although Birinus had probably originally been sent to evangelise the Mercian kingdom further north in the Midlands, he remained with the West Saxons, who he discovered were still pagan. Bede notes that Cynegils embraced the faith after Birinus' preaching and was baptized with his people in 635. This emphasises the corporate nature of conversion, which at this time was a decidedly top-downwards activity.[42]

The dynastic aspect of the conversion should not be underestimated: Oswald, king of Northumbria, acted as Cynegils' sponsor, thereby symbolising peace between the two kingdoms which had frequently been at war in the early years of Cynegils' reign. Oswald was later to marry the king's daughter, which further helped to seal the alliance. Cynegils' son, Cwichelm was baptised in 636 shortly before his death. Cynegils and Oswald gave Birinus the ancient Roman walled settlement of Dorchester for his see, and he is reported as having built and consecrated churches in the surrounding area, although no archaeological evidence survives from this period. Dorchester, like other early foundations including Benson (Bensington) and Abingdon, would have functioned as a Minster, where a community of clergy would have served a large area, perhaps including Cuddesdon.[43] According to Bede, Birinus died in about 642 and was buried in Dorchester.[44] His remains were later translated to Winchester, which soon become a centre of West Saxon power, and which became the seat of the Wessex see around the year 660.[45]

The Anglo-Saxon Charter

From Birinus' time onwards the area around Cuddesdon would have been Christian, although there is no sign of any permanent settlement. By the eighth and ninth centuries, however, there is some evidence from elsewhere of more fixed settlements in the Upper Thames region, but also of continuing struggles between the different English kingdoms. At some point in the eighth century the Upper Thames valley, including the area around Cuddesdon, fell to the kings of Mercia, perhaps after Offa's victory at nearby Benson in 778. It is not clear precisely when the see of Dorchester was re-established as a Mercian see, but a Bishop Ealhheard is mentioned in the Anglo-Saxon Chronicle for the year 897 during the time of Danish conquest of the regions of Mercia further to the north. A Mercian see had previously been established at Leicester, a city which by this time had fallen to Viking invasion. During the tenth century Dorchester re-emerged as an important see under Bishop Ceolwulf, and later Oscytel, who was consecrated in 950, went on to become Archbishop of York, dying at Thame in 971. It was during this period that Cuddesdon was to receive its Charter, although, as has been suggested, there is every likelihood that this merely codified a pattern of ownership which dated back many hundreds of years, perhaps even to the time of Cuthwine himself. In the year 956 King Edwig of England (956-9), granted the vill (the smallest unit of the economic system, often synonymous with 'village' or 'parish') of Cuddesdon (Cuthenes dune) and 20 hides[46] of land to his 'loyal and illustrious Earldorman,' Aelfere.[47] This marks the first definitive evidence for the existence of a settlement in Cuddesdon.

The Royal Charter included a detailed survey of the gift which shows its exact boundaries and gives some indication of land use. These boundaries more or less correspond to the later ecclesiastical parish which lasted until 1852.[48] The boundaries of Cuddesdon included present-day Wheatley as well as small portions of land in Holton and Forest Hill, but did not include either Garsington or Horspath. The first two landmarks mentioned are fords over

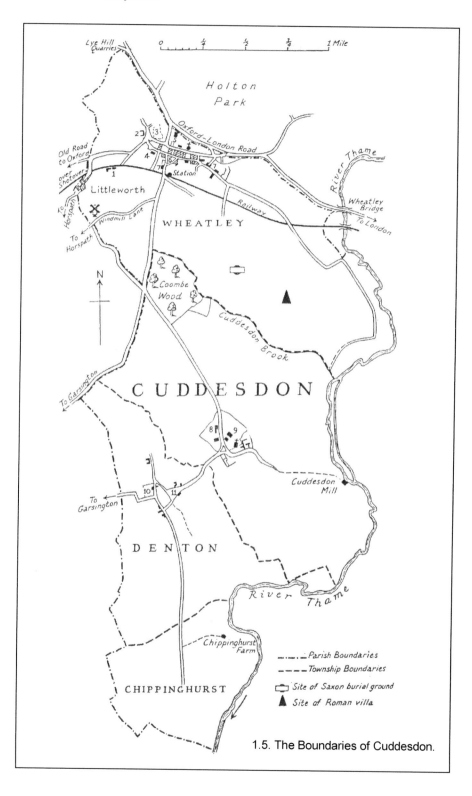

1.5. The Boundaries of Cuddesdon.

the Thame called 'cattle ford' and 'ford in a hollow', and the final landmark is the '*Herepath* ford' or 'ford of the highway' which is located just south of the modern Wheatley Bridge.[49] Other landmarks in the survey cannot be so readily identified. However, at the other side of the parish the name 'dry brook' is still used of a field on the boundary between Denton and Garsington. Next comes 'boundary spring brook' (*Maerwelle*) which survives as Manuall (from a mistake by the Ordnance Surveyers) or Marwell Brook.[50]

From a headland the boundary followed a road (*straet*) which probably still exists as the road running from Wheatley to Garsington.[51] The boundary then led north-west, probably from the cross-roads by Combe Wood,[52] which ran to the headlands, after which the boundary was formed by *Maerweg* (or Boundary way), which Hassall plausibly identified as the boundary path of Shotover Forest. The estate then skirted Wheatley West Field, making its way to a brook probably near the present-day Shotover House. It then ran along *Hlithweg* (or the way of the slope) which was probably alongside Red Hill, to 'the boundary of the religious community', identified as an estate in Forest Hill, which John Blair suggests was most likely to have been the chapelry there of St Frideswide's in Oxford.[53] The boundary then joined with the Islip to Wheatley road at some point near Forest Hill, and stayed with the London Road as far as the highway ford.[54] The approximate area included within these boundaries was 2,805 acres.[55]

Abingdon Abbey and Cuddesdon

At some point before 1066 the estate of Cuddesdon had been transferred to Abingdon Abbey. This marks the beginning of Cuddesdon's long and close association with establishment Christianity. The Abingdon Chronicle claims that, with the permission of King Edwig, Earl Aelfere *immediately* transferred Cuddesdon and its 20 hides 'in pure and perpetual alms to God and the blessed Mary, and the House of Abingdon and the monks therein serving God'.[56] According to Kelly, however, this is a routine statement that is 'unlikely to have any reliable foundation'.[57] Although there are few suspicions about the authenticity of the Charter,[58] there may have been a longer gap between the royal grant to Aelfere and his later grant to the Abbey. Indeed, Cuddesdon may well have been acquired only fairly shortly before the Conquest, since there is evidence of the Abbey building up its endowment in the early eleventh century.[59] On the other hand, it is important to note that around the year 956 Abingdon was undergoing a huge revival under the influence of St Aethelwold (912-84),[60] abbot from 955-63, who re-established the old monastery after a period of neglect, along strict Benedictine lines.[61] For a while Abingdon could lay claim to being the most important monastery in England.

The saint built a new set of convent buildings and an abbey church away from the old minster church of St Helen's. This church had had been founded in the late seventh century (about 675) following a grant of lands by the 'West Saxon under king', Cissa to his kinsman, Haeha, who before the year 709 had become the abbot of a small house of twelve monks.[62] A further tradition speaks of Cissa being joined by his sister, Cilla, both of them obtaining a grant of land from their uncle, one of the under kings of Centwin, which they further endowed from their own resources. Although there is some dispute over the size and importance of the earlier monastery, what is undeniable is that under Aethelwold's influence Abingdon was to become one of the great monasteries of England, comparable with Glastonbury, Bury St Edmund's and St Alban's.[63] Aethelwold's impact on Abingdon, and on the re-establishment of the Benedictine Rule in England through his *Regularis Concordia*, was immense. He had also managed to add considerably to the collection of relics both of local saints and those from further afield. A particularly important possession was the arm, thigh bone, part of a shoulder blade and a rib from the Spanish martyr, Vincent. These had possibly been given to the Abbey by King Eadgar.[64] By 963, when Aethelwold left to become Bishop of Winchester, the monastery at Abingdon was already enormously wealthy.

In relation to the history of Cuddesdon, it is perhaps significant that Aethelwold was made abbot at the command of King Eadred; it is reported that the King's mother, Edgiva, induced him to give Aethelwold the site of the monastery with its forty hides: it is feasible that in building up the abbey's endowment other royal vills would also have been granted over to the abbey.[65] Abingdon continued to receive royal patronage until the Conquest.[66] Since, as has been suggested, Cuddesdon might have been a royal vill, this might indicate an early date for the transfer of the estate to the Abbey.

From the very beginning of its refoundation, the Abbey was closely involved in the administration of its estates.[67] According to Lambrick, Abingdon was a particularly well-managed convent which adopted what was known as the 'living-out' system of estate management, which had first been developed at the great abbey of Cluny in Burgundy.[68] Rather than administering the land centrally, the monks would be directly responsible for management, living out in houses on the estates (*prepositi maneriorum*). This was a system which was apparently unusual in England.[69] It is not clear precisely when Abingdon began this practice, although it is not inconceivable that during the Danish attacks on the area at the beginning of the eleventh century, monks might have been sent out to protect the abbey's landholdings.

It is feasible, therefore, that Cuddesdon would have been administered and served by a monk in its early days as a possession of the abbey.

Although the exact year when Cuddesdon actually passed into the hands of Abingdon Abbey is unknown, it was certainly in its possession by 1066. An interesting incident, mentioned in the Abingdon Chronicle, confirms ownership in that year. The boundary of the Cuddesdon estate always included the mill which lies on the River Thame, and which was later confirmed as property of the Abbey in Faritius's time.[70] The ownership of the mill, an important source of wealth, was the cause of a dispute between the Abbey and the Bishop of Dorchester's tenants at Great Milton. Shortly after the conquest in 1066, after the death of the Saxon Bishop Wulfwig (the last bishop to live and die in the possession of the see of Dorchester before its relocation to Lincoln by the Norman Bishop Remegius in about 1075),[71] a commissioner named Peter, the new Norman king's chaplain (and afterwards Bishop of Lichfield from 1072 (the see of Lichfield was moved briefly to Chester in 1075)) was appointed to inspect the estates of the bishop. These joined with those of Abingdon Abbey at Cuddesdon Mill: there was a long dispute over the ownership of particular courses of water. The last straw came when Peter wanted to destroy a sluice, thereby diverting the course of the water. This so incensed the Saxon Abbot Aldred that arbitration had to be arranged. To argue his case Peter amassed a body of men on his side of the Thame. It looked as if there was going to be a skirmish – but fortunately the abbot brought with him the prized relics of St Vincent whose intercessions evidently proved effective: the Abingdon Chronicle reported (perhaps rather implausibly) that there was a sudden storm and earthquake which only affected the bishop's side of the river. When the horses' hooves began to sink into the ground, the Norman forces started fighting among themselves. The Saxons stood 'on their own feet' watching what was called the 'whirlpool of panic'. Eventually they begged St Vincent to have mercy and the forces withdrew. This divine aid (together with appropriate arbitration) established the right of the Abbot over the Mill. The Chronicle reports that 'after this public demonstration of the virtue of St Vincent, a great impetus to worship in the monastery took place'.[72]

It is not clear whether there have been any more miracles or direct divine interventions in Cuddesdon since that time. The sluice, however, remained a source of dispute and was later twice broken down by the bishop's men, but repaired by the Abbot of Abingdon at his own cost.[73] On two more occasions in 1105 and 1108 the Bishop made his tenants repair it at their own cost.[74] Another dispute in 1284 records a John de Clyfford as having taken a boat, which was the property of the Abbot of Abingdon, from the water at the mill to his house at Milton.[75] In 1272 the mill weir was called 'Cliffware'[76] and in 1397-8 the sacristan of the Abbey gained a revenue of 13s. 4d. from the mill. At the dissolution of the monastery the revenue had fallen to £5.[77]

With the coming of the Norman kings and the huge changes to the religious life Cuddesdon's fortunes, as well as its church, became ever more closely connected with those of the Abbey. The next chapter discusses the origins of the church building and the lengthy disputes over the ecclesiastical income of the parish.

NOTES

1   *Oxford Mail*, 20 January 1956, p. 6.
2   The only effort was by a curate, the Revd E. A. Davies, *Cuddesdon. Its Story*, published privately in 1950. It contains many inaccuracies and some rather wild flights of the imagination. In addition there is an unsigned manuscript in the possession of the Churchwardens dating from about the same time which contains some useful information and a few transcriptions of church records.
3   In 1991 an acheulian axe, shaped some 250,000 years ago, was found in Shotover. On this see the brief summary, 'From Villa to Village: The Roman and Saxon Landscapes' in John Fox (ed.), *One More Millennium: The Story of Wheatley and Holton Park*, Wheatley: 'Wheatley 2000', 2000, pp. 9-11. See also p. 7.
4   'Notice of a Roman villa recently discovered at Wheatley, near Oxford' in *Archaeological Journal* 2 (1846), pp. 350-56. here p. 354. Plates of the find are shown on p. 356. These are copied in *Illustrated London News* 8 (206), 11 April 1846, p. 248.
5   Presumably Bagot, and certainly not William Stubbs, as *VCH* records (i, p. 322). Cf. *Archaeological Journal* 4 (1847), p. 159.
6   *The Berks, Bucks and Oxon Archaeological Journal* 22 (1916), p. 94.
7   *VCH*, i, p. 323. After a talk in the church given in 1850 by Professor Robert Willis of Cambridge, the architectural historian, a party of archaeologists was conducted to Castle Hill to be shown the remains of the Roman villa and hypocaust 'adjacent to the palace' (*Archaeological Journal* 7 (1850), p. 317).
8   *The Berks, Bucks and Oxon Archaeological Journal* 22 (1916), p. 94.
9   Bod. MS Top. Oxon d. 188.
10   *VCH*, i, p. 322.
11   *Journal of Roman Studies* 11 (1921), p. 214. The entry is mistakenly included under Berkshire.
12   John Blair, *Anglo-Saxon Oxfordshire*, Stroud and Oxford: Alan Sutton (Oxfordshire Books), 1994, ch. 1. See also Helena Hamrow, 'Anglo-Saxon Oxfordshire, 400-700' in *Oxoniensia* 64 (1999).
13   E. T. Leeds, 'An Anglo-Saxon Cemetery at Wheatley' in *Proceedings of the Society of Antiquaries* 29 (1916-17), pp. 48-65, here p. 49. It took thirty years or so before the report was published, although a preliminary announcement had been made by J. Kenward in 'A first note on the Anglo-Saxon Cemetery at Wheatley, Oxon' in *Proceedings of the Birmingham Philosophical Society* 4 (1884), p. 179.
14   *VCH* (i, p. 322) gives the number of graves as 46 although no evidence is cited.
15   'An Anglo-Saxon Cemetery at Wheatley', p. 58.
16   Tania M. Dickinson (in *Cuddesdon and Dorchester-on-Thames, Oxfordshire: two early Saxon princely sites in Wessex*, Oxford: British Archaeological Reports, 1974)

discusses the precise location of the find at length. See also Helena Hamrow, 'Anglo-Saxon Oxfordshire, 400-700', pp. 28, 31.

17   *Archaeological Journal* IV (1847), pp. 157-9, here p. 158.

18   J. Y. Akerman, *Remains of Pagan Saxondom*, London: John Russell, 1855, (Vase: Plate VI) pp. 11-12; (Bucket: Plate XIII), pp. 25-6.

19   A brief report appeared in *Oxford Times Limited Edition* Magazine, October 1999, p. 15.

20   The *Antiquaries Journal* 21 (1941), pp. 73-4 (plate facing p. 74) notes a gourd found at Sutton Hoo as closely resembling the Cuddesdon bowls. Martin Conway noted similar finds at Camerton in Somerset (*Proceedings of the Society of Antiquaries* X, p.53). Helena Hamrow, 'Anglo-Saxon Oxfordshire', p. 31.

21   Akerman, *Remains of Pagan Saxondom*, p. 28.

22   Sir Martin Conway, 'Burgundian Buckles and Coptic Influences' in *Proceedings of the Society of Antiquaries* 30 (1918), pp. 63-89, p. 79. G. Baldwin Brown, in *The Arts in Early England* (London: John Murray, 1903-37, vol. 4, pp. 467-9 (pl. 114)) notes that a similar bucket was found at Hexham but makes no claim to Egyptian origin, suggesting instead a Teutonic or provincial Roman manufacture.

23   *Archaeological Journal* IV (1847), p. 158.

24   'The Winchester Anglo-Saxon Bowl' in *Antiquaries Journal* 11 (1931), p. 12. *VCH*, i, p. 322 notes a similar bucket found at Taplow. Plates of the various Cuddesdon finds face p. 355.

25   Blair, *Anglo-Saxon Oxfordshire*, p. 31.

26   Sonia Chadwick Hawkes, 'The Early Saxon Period' in Grace Briggs, Jean Cook and Trevor Rowley (eds), *The Archaeology of the Oxford Region*, Oxford: Oxford University Department for External Studies, 1986, pp. 64-108, here p. 90. See also Barbara Yorke, *Kings and Kingdoms of Early Anglo-Saxon England*, London: Routledge, 1997, pp. 132-56.

27   Dickinson, *Cuddesdon and Dorchester-on-Thames*, p. 11.

28   Dickinson, *Cuddesdon and Dorchester-on-Thames*, p. 21. Radial burials were also found at Shoeburyness and Newport Pagnell (*Archaeological Journal* 77 (1920), p. 282).

29   Dickinson, *Cuddesdon and Dorchester-on-Thames*, p. 23.

30   E. T. Leeds, 'An Anglo-Saxon cemetery at Wheatley', p. 58; cf. Dickinson, *Cuddesdon and Dorchester-on-Thames*, p. 31.

31   Eric John, *Land Tenure in Early England*, Leicester: Leicester University Press, London, 1960.

32   Margaret Gelling, *The Placenames of Oxfordshire*, (2 vols) Cambridge: Cambridge University Press, 1953-4, English Place Names Society (*EPNS*), vols 23, 24.

33   *EPNS* 23, pp. 167-8. Alternatively 'the first element may be, as suggested in the Dictionary of English Place Names, Old English Cuthen, a short form of names in Cuth – formed with the diminutive suffix –in'.

34   *EPNS* 24, p. 267: 'It is not impossible that the man buried here is the one who gave his name to Cuddesdon'. See also Hawkes, 'The Early Saxon Period', p. 90.

35   *EPNS* 23, p. 97.

36   A list of so-called 'c' dynasty leaders is given in Blair, *Anglo-Saxon Oxfordshire*, p. 38. See also Yorke, *Kings and Kingdoms*, pp. 134-5, 143.

37   Dickinson, *Cuddesdon and Dorchester-on-Thames*, p. 33.

38   Hawkes, 'The Early Saxon Period', p. 90. See also Yorke, *Kings and Kingdoms*, pp. 132-4.

39   *Anglo-Saxon Chronicle* (Everyman edition), London: Dent, 1953, pp. 18-19.

40   Hawkes, 'The Early Saxon Period', p. 90. Cf. Blair, *Anglo-Saxon Oxfordshire*, p. 39.

41   Many of the legends surrounding Birinus, most of which are somewhat improbable, are contained in the eleventh-century *Vita Sancti Birini*. Text and translation in Rosalind C. Love (ed.), *Three Eleventh-Century Anglo-Latin Saints' Lives*, Oxford Medieval Texts, Oxford University Press, 1996, pp. 1-47, p. 11. See also J. E. Field, *Saint Berin. The Apostle of Wessex*, London: SPCK, 1902. Margaret Gallyon, *The Early Church in Wessex and Mercia*, Lavenham: Dalton, 1980, pp. 1-9. More generally, see Henry Mayr-Harting, *The Coming of Christianity to Anglo-Saxon England*, London: Batsford, 1972, esp. chs 4 and 6.

42   *Vita Sancti Birini*, p. 35.

43   *Anglo-Saxon Chronicle*, pp. 26-28. On the Minster system, see N. J. G. Pounds, *A History of the English Parish*, Cambridge: Cambridge University Press, 2000, ch. 1.

44   Bede, *Ecclesiastical History*, iii, 7. The *Anglo-Saxon Chronicle* gives the year 650.

45   See also H. E. Salter, 'Ecclesiastical History' in *VCH*, ii, pp. 1-63.

46   Although in theory a hide was 120 acres, it could vary between 60 and 240 acres. By custom it was the land that could be cultivated by one eight ox plough in one year.

47   On Aelfere, see S. E. Kelly (ed.), *Anglo-Saxon Charters*, Oxford: Clarendon Press, 2000, vii, pt. 2, pp. clxxxv-xcii.

48   The original charter is now in the British Library (MS Cotton Augustus ii, 33). It has been printed and translated on a number of occasions: Walter de Gray Birch, *Cartularium Saxonicum* (945), London: Whiting, 1885-1893; John Kemble, *Codex Diplomaticus aevi saxonici*, Londini: Sumptibus Societatis, 1839-1848 (437); G. B. Grundy (ed. and tr.), *Saxon Oxfordshire: Charters and Ancient Highways*, ORS 15, 1933, pp. 18-22. The most modern critical edition is S. E. Kelly (ed.), *Anglo-Saxon Charters*, vii, pt. 2, 'Charters of Abingdon Abbey', pp. 293-298.

49   The clearest account of the boundaries is given in W. O. Hassall (ed.), *Wheatley Records, 956-1056*, ORS 36, 1956, pp. 28-9. See also *VCH*, v, p. 96.

50   *VCH*, v, p. 97.

51   Because of the name '*straet*' Grundy (in *Saxon Oxfordshire*) misinterpreted this to be the Roman Road running from Bicester to Dorchester which still forms the western boundaries of Horspath and Garsington. See Frank Emery, *The Making of the Oxfordshire Landscape*, London: Hodder and Stoughton, 1974, pp. 63-4.

52   On Combe Wood, see Fox, *One More Millennium*, pp. 13-14.

53   Kelly, *Anglo-Saxon Charters*, p. 298.

54   *VCH*, v, pp. 96-8.

55   *VCH*, v, p. 96.

56   Joseph Stevenson, *Chronicon Monasterii de Abingdon*, Rolls Series, 2 vols, vol. i, *From the Foundation of the Monastery Until the Norman Conquest*; vol. ii, *From the Conquest until the accession of Richard I*, London: Longman, 1858, i. pp. 200-203; ii, pp. 513. Hereafter *CMA*.

57   Kelly, *Anglo-Saxon Charters*, p. 296, pp. cxxxii-vi.

58   *CMA*, ii. p. 513.

59   Kelly, *Anglo-Saxon Charters*, p. 296, p. clxiii.

60   On Aethelwold, see Barbara Yorke (ed.), *Bishop Aethelwold: His Career and Influence*, Woodbridge: Boydell, 1988.

61   On Aethelwold and Abingdon, see Alan Thacker, 'Aethelwold and Abingdon' in Yorke (ed.), *Bishop Aethelwold*, pp. 43-64.

62   F. M. Stenton, *The Early History of the Abbey of Abingdon*, Stamford: Paul Watkins, 1989 (reprint), pp. 49-50.

63   Gabrielle Lambrick, 'Abingdon Abbey Administration' in *Journal of Ecclesiastical History* 17 (1966), pp. 159-183, p. 159. Cf. John Hudson (ed.), *Historia Ecclesie Abbendonensis: The History of the Church in Abingdon*, vol. ii, Oxford: Clarendon Press,

2002 (*HEA*), p. lxxxiii. See also D. C. Douglas, 'Some early surveys from the Abbey of Abingdon' in *English Historical Review* 44 (1929), pp. 618-25.

64   Thacker, 'Aethelwold and Abingdon', pp. 59-60.

65   Thacker, 'Aethelwold and Abingdon', pp. 52-3.

66   Emma Cownie, *Religious Patronage in Anglo-Norman England, 1066-1135*, Woodbridge: Boydell for the Royal Historical Society, 1998, pp. 38-9.

67   On the estates of Abingdon, see C. J. Bond, 'The Reconstruction of a Medieval Landscape: the Estates of Abingdon Abbey' in *Landscape History* 1 (1979), pp. 59-75.

68   There is some evidence of the influence of Cluny on Abingdon. See Thacker, 'Aethelwold and Abingdon', p. 54.

69   Lambrick, 'Abingdon Abbey Administration', p. 162. The system may well have ended around the time of the conquest.

70   *CMA*, ii, 288. Cf. *HEA*, p. 172 n. 431.

71   On the see of Dorchester in the eleventh century, see Frank Barlow, *The English Church 1000-1066: A Constitutional History*, London: Longmans, 1963, pp. 215-16.

72   *CMA*, i, 491-2. See also Mieneke Cox *The Story of Abingdon*, Abingdon: Mieneke Cox, 1989, Pt I, pp. 156-7.

73   *HEA*, ii, p. 173; *CMA*, ii, p. 118.

74   *HEA*, ii, p. 173; *CMA*, ii, p. 118.

75   *LC*, p. 349.

76   Hundred Rolls of Edward II, cited in J. H. Parker, *A Guide to the Architectural Antiquities in the Neighbourhood of Oxford*, Deanery of Cuddesdon, Oxford: John Henry Parker, 1846, p. 297.

77   *VCH*, v, p.101. There was another mill mentioned called *Cumbe Brok* in 1279 which seems to have survived until at least 1701. In addition there was a fishery which went with Cuddesdon Mill. Its ownership was included with the manor and eventually passed to Magdalen College.

Chapter Two

Cuddesdon after the Conquest and the Building of the Church

Cuddesdon in Early Norman Times

Following the Norman Conquest there were rapid changes to the monastic houses of England.[1] Both Abingdon and Cuddesdon were profoundly affected by these. During his brief reign, one of King Harold's few ecclesiastical appointments was Abbot Aldred of Abingdon, who after the Conquest quickly submitted to the authority of the new Norman king.[2] It seems that initially this policy proved a success, but after Aldred's support for an unsuccessful rebellion against the King in 1071, the monastery lost several of its estates and was plundered of much of its wealth, particularly by Queen Matilda.[3] Finally, Aldred incurred the King's wrath and was placed in custody by the Bishop of Winchester. The next abbot, Aethelhelm (abbot from 1071-83), a monk of Jumièges, was an efficient administrator. This was particularly important since the abbot was required by the king to supply thirty knights for Windsor; consequently he had to maximise his estate revenue to fulfil this obligation.[4] Aethelhelm managed to ensure the recovery of some estates, but he also lost some other land. This meant that the 557 hides held by the abbey in 1066 had fallen to 374 by the time of Domesday Book in 1086. During his tenure there was also a concerted attempt to purify the Abbey of the marks of its Saxon refounding: even the cult of Aethelwold was prohibited. Aethelhelm's successor, Reginald, managed to ensure increased yields from the Abbey's estates, partly through tightening up the procedure for the collection of tithes.[5]

Throughout this turbulent time, the bulk of the estate at Cuddesdon remained in its hands, although there was a slight decline in hideage from the original gift. The Domesday Book entry for Cuddesdon (*Codesdone*) reported that the Abbey's possessions amounted to land for 18 ploughs. Of these, 4 hides are in demesne, and there are 4 ploughs and 8 serfs; and 24 villeins with 12 borders have 18 ploughs. There is a mill and two fisheries [rendering] 12s. There are 60 acres of meadow, [and] woodland 8 furlongs long and half a league broad. It was worth £9; now £12.[6]

The survey thus also gives some rough idea of the population of the village which must have supported this number of workers. There are 32 serfs and villeins mentioned, plus those who might have worked in the mill, as well as (presumably) those who oversaw the work from the Abbey. There was a male working population of perhaps fifty, which, with women and children, gave a total of perhaps 200.

The fact that no church was mentioned does not prove there was no church building, since Domesday is extremely unreliable in this area. Since there is no archaeological evidence, it is impossible to tell whether there was a church building, although it might be suggested that if a late date is accepted for the granting of the vill to the Abbey, and since it was normal practice for the land-lord to construct a church on his estates, it may well be that the Abbey had not yet set about building a church. However, if an early date is accepted it may well be that a church building had been established. This would probably have been served by the monastic community, and would perhaps have had baptismal and burial rights.

It is, however, certain that a church building existed in Cuddesdon shortly after the Conquest, since in the early twelfth century a church at 'Cudesduna' is mentioned in the will of Faritius, who became Abbot of Abingdon in 1100 after a vacancy of three years serving until his death in 1117.[7] Faritius, who was appointed by Henry I, was from Arezzo and had been a monk at the Benedictine Abbey at Malmesbury. He was skilled as a physician and had served the king and queen in this capacity. Many of his wealthier patients were later to become benefactors of Abingdon Abbey.[8] Faritius' time was a period of unprecedented growth for the Abbey. Numbers of monks had risen from twenty-eight to eighty by the time of his death.[9] The need to accom-modate these larger numbers led to a flurry of building activity in the early part of the twelfth century. It is possible that Cuddesdon's first church, and perhaps also a parsonage house (which is mentioned in the appropriation document of the thirteenth century), was constructed as part of this building programme. The church is mentioned again in 1146 when a bull of Pope Eugenius III confirmed Cuddesdon Church as part of the property of the Abbey which was put under the protection of blessed Peter and himself. In a further bull of 2 April 1152, the Church is confirmed as belonging to the Abbey.[10]

Faritius also succeeded in recovering 47 hides of the Abbey's estates, as well as securing many further grants of land. He also added to the Abbey's collection of relics with a number of Anglo-Saxon bones including the shoulder blades of both Aldhelm and Wilfrid: it seems that the English saints were back in favour.[11] At the same time, however, the increasing secularisation of the personal obligations to the abbot, who in many ways functioned as a feudal lord, as well as his various military obligations, put further pressure on the Abbey's finances. This meant that there was a growing need to ensure the efficient administration both of the estates and the abbot's household. Faritius consequently set about increasing the Abbey's income: new grants of all kinds were quickly bestowed on the monastery including various royal privileges, tithes, portions, rents and estates. Older sources of income and their corresponding charters were confirmed, codified and collected together in a single set of authoritative legal documents: it is likely that this applies to the various pensions and tithes accruing from the estate of Cuddesdon, which are noted in a bull of confirmation of Innocent III to Abbot Hugh dated 7 March 1200/1.[12] An similar act of Hugh of Avalon, Bishop of Lincoln, dated 16 November 1200, confirms to the possession of the Abbey 'pensions from churches and tithes from the archdeaconry of Oxford' including 'the whole village of Cuddesdon'.[13] Faritius is also reported as having rebuilt Cuddesdon mill which had been destroyed 'in tempore Danorum'.[14] In addition to the income from its estates, the Abbey also received pensions from over twenty churches, including Cuddesdon, to which it also held the right of presentation. It was also noted in the Cartulary that some of the tithe income of Cuddesdon parish was also due to the Abbey, together with the tithes of one hide held by Richard Gernun in Wheatley.[15]

Domesday Book also mentions another manor within the old charter boundaries of Cuddesdon at Chippinghurst (*Cibbaherste*). Since this was held 'of the king' by the Norman Count of Evreux, the land had evidently been lost by the monastery shortly after the Conquest and had become royal property. The manor comprised three hides: 'Of this land 2 hides are in demesne, and there are 2 ploughs, with 1 serf; and 4 villeins have 2 ploughs. There are 24 acres of meadow. It was and is worth 40s.' Not long afterwards, in 1108, William, Count of Evreux and Helewis, his wife, founded the priory of Noyon, to which they donated all their English lands, including Chippinghurst.[16] It is noteworthy that Abingdon, which had been the one of the most important recipients of gifts in Berkshire and much of Oxfordshire, was facing competition in the early twelfth century from new monasteries at home and abroad, notably Reading, founded by Henry I, and Oseney, founded by Robert D'Oilly in 1129. In the reign of Edward I, the manor of

Chippinghurst was still held by the Prior of Noyon, the valuation of 1291 under Pope Nicholas showing an income of £6.[17] In 1316, during the reign of Edward II, it was held by 'Domina Benedicta de Chibberhurst'.[18] Noyon remained overlord, however, until it was deprived in 1414 by Henry V, who gave the manor to the royal foundation of Sheen, which retained it until the sixteenth century. Chippinghurst seems to have been administered by tenants throughout this period.

Other land in the parish of Cuddesdon was also held by religious houses: a Foundation Charter of Henry I of 1122[19] granted 12 thraves in Chippinghurst and 3 acres of wheat in Cuddesdon as well as 4 thraves in Denton to the Augustinian prior and convent of S. Frideswide in Oxford (which became Christ Church after the dissolution). It would seem that over the years this gift was much disputed: on 8 January 1140/1 Pope Innocent II gave a charter of general confirmation.[20] In 1142 the Empress Maud again confirmed the 1122 gift, as did Pope Adrian IV on 26 February 1157/8.[21] The process was repeated by the Bishop of Lincoln, William of Blois, on 12 August 1203 and 10 May 1206.[22] After an inquiry into the right of the Prior to possess land in Cuddesdon, a verdict was given in his favour on 9 August 1324, which reveals that there was still doubt as to the authenticity of the original gift after over two hundred years.[23] Bishop Thomas of Lincoln again confirmed the gift in 1344. It should be noted that these disputes occurred at a time when Oxfordshire was one of the wealthiest counties in England and when land was a particularly valuable commodity.[24] Elsewhere in the ancient parish of Cuddesdon, in about 1240 two hides in Denton and one in Wheatley passed to the Templars when they received the manor of Sandford.[25] Wheatley, which was first mentioned as a separate manor in 1135,[26] grew substantially during the middle ages: by 1377 there were 110 people over fourteen registered for the Poll Tax.

The First Period of the Building of the Church

There is no precise information as to the exact date when work commenced on the present church building in Cuddesdon. Following James Parker's 1846 guide, architectural historians have given a date of about 1180 principally on account of the pointed arches in the crossing as well as the decoration around the west doorway.[27] This would fit in well with the consolidation of the rectory with the abbey, but it is also possible that the date of the church is a little earlier, since styles were already changing by 1180. The dating is far from certain: it is perhaps noteworthy that Faritius had been a monk at Malmesbury where pointed arches were used much earlier in the

Mouldings of Arch of West Door.

Left 2.1. West Door (1846) **Right** 2.2. West Door Mouldings. From Parker's *Guide*

twelfth century. It is quite likely that the building made use of masons from the Abbey which was involved in building work on its conventual buildings at about the same time.[28] If 1180 or thereabouts is accepted, this would place it during the abbacy of Roger (1175-85), who had previously been prior of Bermondsey, and who was described in the Abingdon Chronicle as 'cruel and suspicious'.[29]

It is highly likely that the new cruciform church was built on the site of the earlier church mentioned in Faritius' will. The only possible evidence of the earlier church is some fragments of indented mouldings, taken from an arch, built into the walls of the south transept and the tower. Although these may come from the earlier structure, it would seem far more likely that they come from a subsequent restoration: the exposed position makes the church particularly susceptible to weathering, especially on the south side, and good quality faced stone was always likely to have been recycled.

From its beginnings Cuddesdon church was a relatively large building suited to its commanding position overlooking both the Chilterns and the Berkshire Downs. There are several features of the present structure which almost certainly date from the initial period of building. The most notable is the fine and impressive west doorway, together with the ironwork on the door itself (which is an interesting attempt at two-dimensional foliage). The round arch of the doorway comprises three richly carved orders, the inner plain, the middle with a roll-moulding and dog-tooth decoration, the outer with a band of lozenges with cut-out centres under a hood with beasts' head stops, which Parker describes as a 'very good specimen of the latest Norman work'.[30] Mr

2.3. West Door Pillasters (MC)

Rooke and Mr Freeman reported on a visit to Cuddesdon for the Oxford Architectural Society in 1844 that the 'mouldings on the west doorway are very remarkable, shewing the change from the Norman zigzag to the Early English ornament'.[31] This was re-iterated later by Jennifer Sherwood who thought that the capitals of the jamb shafts offer 'an instructive example of the transition from Late Norman stylised upright leaves to something approaching freer Early English stiff-leaf'.[32] The south doorway, which was presumably moved to its present position when the aisles were built in the following century, also probably dates from the foundation of the church. It offers another example of the transition from Norman to Early English, containing two orders, the inner plain, and the outer with bands of roll-moulding and dogtooth. The capitals on the jamb shaft are carved with embryo stiff-leaf and a head on the east side.

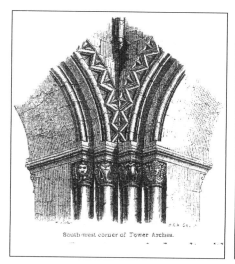

South-west corner of Tower Arches.

Left 2.4. South-west corner of Tower Arches from Parker's *Guide*
Right 2.5. Detail from Tower Arch (MC)

2.6. Blocked door (MC)

The substantial supporting arches of the tower with their elaborate carving provide another important feature dating from the original period. These arches are undoubtedly the most impressive and striking feature of the church interior: the outer faces of the arch have two orders with angle half-rolls, except the arch facing the nave, which has a hood with doghead stops, an outer order of zigzag, and an inner order which has a roll-moulding. The inner orders of all four arches are similar, the outer order with a band of zigzag and an angle roll, the inner plain with an angle roll. The capitals of the jamb shafts are fluted on the east, but on the west there are beasts' heads, waterleaf and crocket capitals. Parker also describes the corbels as the only remains of the stone vault under

2.7. West wall buttresses (MC)
2.8. Norman Window in North Transept from Parker's *Guide*

the tower, which may well have been lower than the present Victorian restoration.

It is also likely that the blocked opening in the tower, together with the string course underneath, is part of the original building.[33] Most commentators have assumed this was a door to a rood loft. However, since roods developed much later than 1180, this is unlikely, even if a rood was constructed at some later stage in the church's history. Given the length of the chancel and the physical separation of the nave, it is feasible that the church was designed to house a daughter house of Abingdon Abbey.[34] The font, which stands on a Victorian pedestal, is a typical large plain barrel shaped one of the same period: the adze marks of the masons can be clearly seen. On the exterior of the church a relatively unusual feature are the small Norman buttresses at the west end (which are repeated in the east and west corners of the north transept).

Most of the walls of the north transept, together with the blocked door on the east side and the round-arched window, also probably date from this initial period. The stone seating around the south transept, which is also likely to have extended around the north transept, since some remains are still visible,[35] probably dates from the first period of building. Evidence of the

2.9. North Aisle showing buttress Remnant of Original Nave (MC)

original aisleless church can be seen in the original corbel table inside the roof of the later aisle roofs on both north and south sides, as well as the somewhat surprising remains of the upper parts of the pilaster buttresses inside the church. Also clearly visible are outlines of a clerestory beneath the corbel table on the north side.

Other parts of the church are more difficult to date. The west porch, which has become badly weathered, may possibly be part of the original church, or built within twenty or thirty years after its construction. However, following Parker, Davies, placed it in the fourteenth century at the same time as the south porch.[36]

The Income from Cuddesdon

Alongside such building work both in Abingdon and on its estates, the early twelfth century saw a re-organisation of the structures of the monastery with various officers appointed to look after the different aspects of the monastery's life.[37] The income from Cuddesdon was considered so central that one of the monks was given the title 'reeve' or 'keeper of Cuddesdon'. This was an additional obedientary to the more usual monastic offices which had been set up in Faritius's time. During Abbot Vincent's time (1121-30), £4 from the 'reeveship' of Cuddesdon was used to 'buy wine from which the brethren are to have their special allowance on the main feast days'. Similarly, 60s. from the rents of Cuddesdon and Charney was to be used for the provision of fuel for the brothers.[38] The main duty of the keeper of Cuddesdon continued to be the provision of the convent, including herrings, eggs and fowls, but especially wine for the cellarer to be used at thirty special festivals, which are mentioned from 1189 to 1221.[39] These goods were bought with 30s. from the Cuddesdon tithe, 20s. from the custom of the office, and with

Upper Section of Wall of North Aisle, shewing Buttress cut away.

Junction of last Arch of North Aisle, with opening to Roodloft.

2.10. North Aisle showing buttress Remnant and Clerestory and blocked door to rood loft (before restoration) from Parker's *Guide*

various other monies earmarked from the profits of the manor.[40] On 13 October 1288, it was noted that Abbot Richard gave the keeper of Cuddesdon a horse and a servant in return for feeding two hundred paupers on the anniversary of his appointment.[41] Not surprisingly, given its large yield, the estate of Cuddesdon is frequently mentioned in the accounts of the Obedientiars of Abingdon: in 1375/6, for instance, the Abbey received £66 and in 1383, £86 from the Cuddesdon estates, both very large sums at the time.[42] The accounts also mention regular payments 'to the poor of Cuddesdon' in return.[43] In 1375/6 and 1383/4, for instance, this amounted to £2 16s. 8d.[44]

This preoccupation with administration, together with the relatively large sums of money involved, led to frequent conflicts between the abbot and his monks. It is interesting to note that the revenues of Cuddesdon were handed over to the convent by Abbot Hugh after one such period of conflict in the early thirteenth century. Cuddesdon manor was eventually confirmed as the property of the convent rather than the abbot before Richard Poore, Bishop of Salisbury, in 1220.[45] Other conflicts over the income accruing from Cuddesdon, particularly from the church, went far beyond the shores of England, as will be shown in the next chapter.

NOTES

1   On this, see Frank Barlow, *The English Church, 1066-1154*, London: Longmans, 1979, pp. 177-216.

2   *CMA*, i, p. 482.

3   *CMA*, i, p. 484, 485-93. See Cownie, *Religious Patronage*, p. 39, and introduction to *Historia Ecclesie Abbendonensis: The History of the Church in Abingdon*, ii, ed. John Hudson, Oxford: Clarendon Press, 2002. (*HEA*).

4   *VCH*, v, p. 109. Abingdon's obligations seem to have been about average, although some similar houses owed far less including St Augustine's, Canterbury. See Cownie, *Religious Patronage*, p. 41; and Lambrick, 'Abingdon Abbey Administration' p. 164-5. See *HEA*, pp. lviii-lxv. A writ of Henry I in Faritius' time shows the difficulties experienced in enforcing this service. See *HEA*, p. 132.

5   Cownie, *Religious Patronage*, p. 43.

6   John Morris (ed.), *Domesday Book 14: Oxfordshire Parallel Latin text and English translation*, Chichester: Phillimore, 1978. The woodland mentioned is presumably Combe Wood. For the later history of Combe Wood, see *VCH*, v, p. 98. The bulk of Abingdon's estates were in Berkshire. Abingdon's other Oxfordshire estates included land at Lewknor.

7   *HEA*, ii, p. 215; *CMA*, ii, p. 192. Cf. Parker, *Guide*, p. 296. Mention is also made of churches at St Martin in Oxford, Marcham, Uffington, Wittenham, and Nuneham.

8   *HEA*, i, p. xlvi. Cownie, *Religious Patronage*, p. 46.

9   *CMA*, ii, p. 287. See *HEA*, pp. c-civ.

10   *HEA*, p. 267; *CMA*, ii, 196. Cf. Parker, p. 296.

11   Cownie, *Religious Patronage*, pp. 46-8.

12   C. R. and M. G. Cheney (eds.), *Letters of Innocent III, 1198-1216 concerning England and Wales*, Oxford: Clarendon, 1967, p. 49 (296).

13   *English Episcopal Acta (Lincoln)*, vol. iv, pp. 3-4.

14   *CMA*, ii. p. 288. Cf. ii, p. 118. If the mill was destroyed in the time of the Danes it is difficult to see how the story of the skirmish in 1066 could be true.

15   *LC*, p. 24.

16   On this see *VCH*, v, p. 107.

17   T. Astle, S. Ayscough and J. Caley (eds), *Taxatio Ecclesiastica Angliae et Walliae auctoritate p. Nicholai IV, circa A.D. 1291* (19 Edward I), London: Record Commission, 1802, p. 30. The same note includes confirmation of the estate at 'Quotesdon, Denton and Whatele' as owned by the Abbot of Abingdon.

18   Francis Palgrave (ed.), *Nomina Villarum*, (Parliamentary Writs, Writs of Military Summons), London: Public Records Commission, 1834, ii, div. 3 f. 353.

19   S.R. Wigram (ed.), *The Cartulary of the Monastery of St. Frideswide at Oxford* (hereafter *SFC*), Oxford: Oxford Historical Society, 28, 1895 (vol. i) & 31, 1896 (vol. ii), here, i, pp. 10-11.

20   *SFC*, i, p. 22. Years were usually reckoned from Lady Day – 25th March.

21   *SFC*, i, pp. 11, 28.

22   David Smith (ed.), *English Episcopal Acta (Lincoln)*, iv, Oxford: Oxford University Press, 1986, p. 173. The confirmation records one acre each of wheat, rye and oats in Cuddesdon, 12 thraves of corn in Chippinghurst and four in Denton.

23   *SFC*, ii, pp. 201-2.

24   In 1334 a new basis of taxation saw Oxford yielding 38s. 10d. per thousand acres. See also Hilary L. Turner, *Oxfordshire. A Look at the Past*, Derby: Plotwood Press, 1997, p. 42.

25   Agnes M. Leys (ed.), *The Sandford Cartulary*, ORS 19, 1938, i, p. 4.

26   On Wheatley see W. O. Hassall (ed.), *Wheatley Records, 956-1056.*

27   Parker, *Guide*, p. 288.

28   M. Biddle, Gabrielle Lambrick, J. N. L. Myers, 'The Early History of Abingdon, Berkshire, and its Abbey' in *Medieval Archaeology* 12 (1968) pp. 26-69.

29   *CMA* ii, p. 293.

30   Parker, *Guide*, p. 290.

31   *Oxford Architectural Society Meeting*, 1 May 1844, p. 5f.

32   Nikolaus Pevsner and Jennifer Sherwood, *The Buildings of England: Oxfordshire*, Harmondsworth: Penguin, 1974, p. 562.

33   Parker, *Guide*, p. 291.

34   I owe this suggestion to Professor Diarmaid MacCulloch.

35   Parker, *Guide*, p. 291. They are still visible but partly obscured by the organ.

36   Parker, *Guide*, p. 292.

37   Lambrick, 'Abingdon Abbey Administration', pp. 167-8.

38   *HEA*, p. 253.

39   *CMA*, ii, pp. 312, 314-17 lists the feast days when wine would have been provided.

40   *CMA*, ii, p. 322.

41   *CC*, p. 236. See also p. 54.

42   *VCH*, v, p. 101.

43   *CC*, p. 227. Lambrick, 'Abingdon Abbey Administration', p. 169. *CMA*, ii, 172, 293, 307-8, 314, 322-5. The revenues, and possibly the produce of Cuddesdon were put into the service of the kitchener in a settlement of about 1185 (*CMA*, ii, 307, 323).

44   R. E. G. Kirk (ed.), *Accounts of the Obedientiars of Abingdon Abbey*, London: Camden Society, 1891-2, p. 44.

45   *CC*, p. 226. This was confirmed by a papal bull of 12 June 1220 (*LC*, pp. 30-1).

Chapter Three

The Later Middle Ages: Finance and the Expansion of the Church

Conflict over the Church Revenues

The parish system as we know it today developed over a lengthy period in the years before and after the Norman Conquest as landowners built churches to serve their estates. This meant that the minster system, where priests served a number of settlements from a central base, was gradually displaced by a network of local parish churches built in most communities of any size. These parish churches were often treated as part of the property of the landowner, who, as patron, had the right to present a clergyman to minister in the church (the 'advowson'). Indeed bishops often had little control over the appointment of the clergyman. Such churches were usually endowed with gifts of land (the 'glebe') as well as the flat rate ten per cent ecclesiastical tax on all the produce of the land (the 'tithe'). Initially, it would seem, these gifts had been collected by the patron who in turn paid the clergyman,[1] but gradually they became due to the holder ('incumbent') of the ecclesiastical office ('benefice'). Some security of tenure was thereby given to the clergyman, who, in the days of clerical marriage, would often hand down the benefice to his descendants. Since they were often valuable commodities there was also much buying and selling of ecclesiastical benefices.[2]

In a period when the papacy and the church were increasingly trying to assert their power over the laity, there were many efforts to improve the situation. For instance, private patronage was condemned at the First Lateran Council in 1123 with the injunction that 'priests are to be appointed to parish churches by the bishops'. Similarly, the outlawing of clerical marriage at the Second Lateran Council in 1139 was directed against the inheritance of benefices, and the Third Lateran Council of 1179 condemned the sale of benefices as the sin of simony. In England the system of patronage that eventually emerged meant that the patron had the right to present the clergyman, but only if the bishop was prepared to institute him and his representative (usually the archdeacon) induct him into the benefice. The right of presentation remained an important and valuable privilege and became a way of distributing offices among family members of church or royal office holders: advowsons continued to be bought and sold until the nineteenth century. Even to this day they can be inherited. There were frequent disputes about the ownership of the advowson, which was treated as a piece of property like any other. However, after it was clear that the ecclesiastical revenues were due to the incumbent there was usually little direct financial benefit for the patron.[3]

Rectors and Vicars

In economic terms it was the income from the benefice itself that was far more important than the advowson. From the time of Urban II (1088-99) the papacy made efforts to ensure that the totality of the income from the benefice was diverted to ecclesiastical use, since there were many objections to the diversion to the laity of money which had been 'given to God' to provide for ministry. Consequently it was during the twelfth century that the term 'rector' began to be used of those incumbents to whom the whole of the income of the benefice was to be directed. However, these rectors were sometimes non-resident and would pay for their spiritual duties to be undertaken by a chaplain. At the same time many religious houses began to receive gifts of benefices, so that the income would be diverted towards the finances of the monastery. This meant that the income 'given to God', which usually consisted primarily of tithes, was redirected away from the parish towards the religious house. This practice was termed 'appropriation' and required episcopal approval. This meant that the head of the house, or sometimes the monastery collectively, assumed the responsibilities of the 'rector' of the parish.[4]

Given that there were obligations to perform certain ecclesiastical functions in the parish, a clergyman was instituted into the parish as a representative ('vicar') of the rector. He would assume the cure of souls and have the right to a certain portion of the income of the benefice which was ordained by the bishop. Following the ruling of the Third Lateran Council of 1179 the vicar could not be removed by the rector of the parish and had absolute claim to his portion of the benefice.[5] Usually the vicar's portion was made up of the so-called 'lesser' tithes (like chickens and lambs) which were difficult to collect, as well as some of the glebe. In general the rector had the right to the greater tithes (for example, wheat and oats). Detailed legal documents were frequently drawn up specifying the precise portions paid to rector and vicar.

The Rectory of Cuddesdon and 'Papal Provision'

It is possible that the rectory of Cuddesdon was first established in Abbot Faritius' time, but it is not until the latter part of the twelfth and early thirteenth centuries that the names of any rectors are mentioned. It is almost certain that the early rectors were non-resident, ministry being undertaking by 'chaplains'. Indeed the first clergyman mentioned as ministering in Cuddesdon was a 'Robert[us]' who was described as 'capellanus de Cudesdune', and who in 1189 witnessed a document which appears in the cartulary of Oseney Abbey.[6] Shortly afterwards, various documents relating to Abingdon Abbey give the names of three early rectors, two Johns and their predecessor, Nicholas in the early years of the thirteenth century.

It might at first sight seem surprising that the two Johns should have been Italian cardinals. The explanation, however, is probably relatively straightforward. Although it was not common, the practice of instituting Italians to English benefices was certainly not unknown elsewhere in England. After the reforms of the eleventh century, the papacy was increasing in power, and the resulting bureaucracy meant that wealthy benefices from across the Western Church were in demand to provide income for Vatican officials. The means by which this was put into effect was that the traditional rights of presentation were usurped by the papacy, which in turn nominated a clergyman of its own choice. This practice was termed 'papal provision' (and was later outlawed in England through the Statutes of Provisors in the fourteenth century). In the thirteenth century, as will be shown, it frequently led to lengthy legal dispute between the patron and the pope, especially when the benefice itself was being sought after by a religious house. The lengthy proceedings, however, often meant that by the time all the disputes had been settled, there was little material gain by the religious house.

Given that the papacy of Innocent III (1198-1216) was an important period in the increasing assertion of papal authority, it is feasible that the granting of relatively wealthy English benefices like Cuddesdon to senior Italian clergy was instigated by papal provision: as Cheney notes, most Italian rectors of English benefices were nephews of popes or curial officials.[7] Since the advowson of Cuddesdon was vested in Abingdon, it is feasible that the pope commanded the Abbey to nominate his own choice, perhaps in return for certain favours at the papal court.[8] It is also possible, however, that the Italians were the abbot's own nominees, since they might well have proved helpful in upholding his causes in Rome – it is impossible to know the precise lines of appointment.

The Appropriation of the Rectory

As noted in the previous chapter there was a decline in the landed wealth of Abingdon Abbey after the Conquest, which, together with the rising levels of feudal obligation, meant that it became increasingly important to secure new sources of revenue for the Abbey. These included the appropriation of rectories, including those on its own estates. At the beginning of the thirteenth century, however, only two of the Abbey's parish churches were served by vicars, which probably indicates that Abingdon had not yet adopted the practice of appropriating rectorial income (the 'rectory').[9] However, a century later in 1309, the income of five churches, including Cuddesdon, had been made over to the Abbey, and another (Uffington) was acquired in 1344. Not surprisingly, it was usually the wealthiest churches that were appropriated first.

The process of the appropriation of Cuddesdon was particularly long and complicated primarily because of its non-resident Italian rectors. Indeed, something of the complexities of international ecclesiastical power politics and the broader issues between pope, bishop and state which emerged in the thirteenth century can be demonstrated in the various disputes involving the revenues of the benefice and the appropriation of Cuddesdon rectory to the Abbey. In the first years of the thirteenth century there was a long and complex dispute between the Abbot and the Rector of Cuddesdon, at the time John, Cardinal Deacon of SS. Cosmas and Damian, over the rights to certain tithes of Cuddesdon church.[10] The Abbot was already making a claim to some of the tithe income from Cuddesdon church, which was the subject of a papal bull of 7 March 1200/1.[11] A mandate was issued to the papal legate in September 1208 to hear the case.[12] A further mandate was issued on 2 January 1209 to restore the tithes to the cardinal within three months unless the Abbot could prove his rights to them. The cardinal was also to be given 60 marks worth of goods in respect of the tithes withheld, and the tithe income was ordered to be restored to the cardinal's proctor, Mr W. de Moy.[13] 'After due process,' it was noted in the Chatsworth Cartulary, 'an amicable agreement was made between the parties, viz. that cardinal John should have them as long as he held Cuddesdon (Codesdon) church, as Nicholas his predecessor had them, rendering, as had Nicholas, 40s. yearly to the abbot and convent ... which 40s. anyone holding the church in the cardinal's name would pay.'[14] The attestations and the papal ruling dated 21 May 1210 were deposited in the strong-room of Oseney duly sealed to safeguard future rights.[15] The Abbey was thus confirmed in a proportion of the income of the benefice, although it had not yet succeeded in appropriating the whole of the rectorial income.

Later in the century the Abbey continued in its efforts to appropriate the living, seeking the resignation of the next rector, another cardinal, John de Colonna, who may well have been related to Stephen de Collona, Rector of St Helen's, Abingdon, and who may feasibly have been a papal nominee. It is possible that this John was also a relative of Peter de Colonna, who was made a canon of Lincoln 'at the instance and petition of Innocent III'.[16] By 1231 John had agreed to resign, which would have made possible the appropriation of the rectory of Cuddesdon.[17] The following year the indult (*indulgemus*) for the granting of the rectory to the Abbey was made by Pope Gregory IX (dated 3 March 1232). It instructed that the income was to be used to help with the maintenance of sick monks and a proportion was to be held back for a vicar to undertake pastoral ministry. The indult reads:

> For the greater exercise of their works of piety and as an expression of papal thanks for the devotion shown to him in the person of John, cardinal priest of St Pressede the pope, approving the supplications of the same John, grants, by the authority of these presents, that they be allowed to convert to their own uses the church of Cuddesdon (*Codesdon*), held by John from their monastery in whose gift it lies, after the decease or renunciation of the same, for the maintenance of sick (*infirmancium*) monks; a suitable portion being reserved to the vicar according to the resources of the same church, so that he can sustain the burdens, and neither the diocesan bishop nor the same church be defrauded of due services.[18]

Gregory issued a mandate (also dated 3 March 1232) to Hugh of Welles, Bishop of Lincoln, in whose diocese Cuddesdon fell, instructing him that the abbot and convent would be allowed to appropriate the rectory of Cuddesdon after the departure of John.[19] Hugh, it should be noted, established no fewer than 174 vicarages.[20] In this case, however, he refused to implement the papal mandate for induction, which meant that the dispute continued. A further papal letter of 30 April 1235 to the bishop, treasurer and chancellor of Salisbury, in whose diocese and under whose jurisdiction Abingdon fell, ordered the bishop of Lincoln to induct the abbot and convent into Cuddesdon Church, and if he still refused, the bishop of Salisbury would be required to do so, without the possibility of appeal.[21]

In the meantime the cardinal rector of Cuddesdon had raised his price for vacating the rectory, which was necessary before the appropriation could take place; the terms eventually agreed on included the payment of a pension to him by the Abbey.[22] This meant that on 2 May 1235 Pope Gregory gave another indult to the Abbey concerning the appropriation of the Cuddesdon rectory for the use of sick monks, 'saving fitting maintenance for a perpetual vicar there who would respond to the diocesan bishop concerning episcopal rights'. However, 'to avoid their being defrauded by malice, he now, at the supplication of the said cardinal, allows them to appropriate the said church, having assigned to the cardinal a fitting annual pension from the goods of the monastery elsewhere'.[23] The dispute, however, lingered on: the bishop of Salisbury had evidently also refused to induct the abbot into the Rectory.

In the end recourse was made to Otho, Gregory's cardinal legate, who received a letter from the Pope dated 1 July 1237 mandating him to induct the abbot and convent if the bishops still refused.[24] The induction finally took place on 15 December 1237 at Liddington (*Lydington*) in 1237 after Robert Grosseteste (who was deeply critical of the practice of appropriation) had replaced Hugh as bishop.

> He has, by papal authority, instituted the abbot and convent of Abingdon into Cuddesdon (*Codesdon*) church as rectors and had them inducted into corporeal possession of the same, saving the vicarage, assessed by Mr Roger de Weseham, archdeacon Oxonie, the vicar being instituted on presentation to the bishop by the abbot and convent.[25]

Although it is not clear whether the appropriation of Cuddesdon rectory was worth all the effort, it is nevertheless true more generally that the revenues drawn from its churches contributed greatly to Abingdon's vast wealth, helping it become the sixth richest religious house in the country by the time of the dissolution.[26] The money from Cuddesdon Church was quickly put to use by the monastery. In 1247, ten years after the appropriation of the rectory, the convent agreed to pay £40 to Hugh fitz Henry from Cuddesdon Church for lands bought in Abingdon.[27] Valuations of the rectory record £20 for the Valuation of Norwich of 1254,[28] and £26 13s. 4d. in 1291 for the taxation of Pope Nicholas IV who sought to raise money for what turned out to be an abortive crusade.[29] It remained unchanged in 1341.[30]

The Vicarage of Cuddesdon

The archdeacon's extremely detailed assessment of the endowment of the vicarage was made shortly after the induction of the abbot into the rectory. The vicar was to receive the altar dues or fees (*altaragium*) of the church, half a hide of land at Denton with adjoining meadow and common pasture, and pastorage for 4 draught animals (*averiorum*) and 2 young bullocks (*stottorum*), with the animals themselves belonging to Abingdon Abbey. In addition he received the whole croft (*crofta*) to the dwelling house (*ad mansum*) of the vicar near the cemetery of the said church on the north near the dwelling house once of the parson of the same church near the cemetery on the north side of Cuddesdon church. … [He had all the] tithes of hay and all other tithes and obventions pertaining to the said church, except tithes of the mills and all small tithes of hay from the demesne of the said monks, and all tithes of sheaves that the said monks will wholly have, and except for a part of the said croft for a road (*viam*) 12 ft. wide along which the said monks can carry their corn. The vicar will personally minister in the said church and will find suitable assistants (*ministros ydoneos*), books, ornaments and effective lights (*compencia luninaria*), and will sustain episcopal and archidiaconal burdens. The assessment is reckoned at 20 marks, and has been registered in the small journal (*iurnicula*) of the bishop of Lincoln.[31]

Two years after the rectory had been granted to Abingdon Abbey a priest named Richard ('capellanus') was presented by the Abbey and Convent of Abingdon and instituted to the perpetual vicarage in 1239, becoming the first vicar of Cuddesdon.[32] The value of the vicarage seems to have declined rapidly after its foundation, falling to a mere £4 for the Valuation of Norwich in 1254[33] and £5 6s. 8d. for the Papal Taxation of 1291.[34] However, in a collation made on 2 April 1353 by Bishop John Gynewell the vicarage was said to be worth once again 20 marks (£13 6s. 8d.).[35] By this time one-third of all English livings had been appropriated by religious houses, with only about one-quarter worth more than £15 per annum.

The Second Period of Building

In about 1240, perhaps in response to the appropriation of the rectory and the establishment of the vicarage, work was begun on the expansion of the church building: nave aisles were added rather clumsily on both north and south sides. The manner of construction was relatively unusual.[36] The building of the aisles provoked a lengthy discussion among members of the Oxford Architectural Society, thirty of whom visited Cuddesdon on 16 March 1878, to be shown around the Church by the vicar, C. W. Furse. 'The most interesting feature of the church', it was noted, was the construction of the aisles '*apparently by piercing the Norman walls*'.[37] This raised the question 'whether it were possible, or if possible, profitable, so to pierce the walls and leave the upper portion intact'. There was evidently a heated discussion with James Parker (author of the 1846 architectural guide to the Cuddesdon deanery) thinking it 'scarcely likely' that so much trouble would be taken for

3.1. North Aisle from the crossing (MC)

such a small portion of wall, since it would have been much easier to have simply demolished the wall and started again (although that would presumably have meant re-roofing the nave). Mr Burton and Mr Barns, on the other hand, suggested that remains of the buttresses and the corbel table could not have appeared if the wall had been demolished. They consequently thought

3.2. Lancet windows in south wall (MC)

that the arches would have been completed alongside the aisles of the church, and thrown open only when finished, by removing the wall masonry between the inserted arches. It was noted that the same had been done on the south-west aisle of Dorchester Abbey. Such were the debates with which the late Victorian architect was occupied. The rough bases of some of the pillars indicate that these may even have been shaped from the original stonework. The second theory seems more plausible, although it is remarkable that there was never any proper making good: this may perhaps suggest an abrupt halt to the rebuilding, presumably for financial reasons.

The aisles consist of a plain three bay arcade with octagonal piers with vigorously moulded projecting capitals of varying quality. Some of the arches have a string moulding above and some are plain, again indicating an abrupt halt to the construction. The aisles themselves are typically Early-English with lean-to roofs. Originally they had very low side-walls: the roofs were consequently much steeper than at present. A close examination of the different masonry in the west wall of the south aisle reveals that the height was not much higher than the low buttresses on the outside walls of the aisles. The original low aisles were probably lit by a number of small lancet windows, since three are still in place on the wall of the south aisle, and one each at the western end of both aisles. The simple north doorway also probably dates from this time, as do the 'elegant little' corbels on the west side of the tower arch which carried the rood loft.[38]

The Third Period of Building

3.3. West wall showing evidence of roof extension (MC)

In about 1350 the low walls of the aisles were raised and the larger decorated windows added on the north side, probably in place of earlier lancets.[39] Parker also suggests that the 'small window, of the time of Edward I, was removed and built into the new work above the three small lancet windows on the south side'.[40] It is not clear, however, that the present window is of this date. The exterior masonry and the shape of the interior indicate that there may at some point have been a different shaped window, which perhaps dated from the seventeenth century, possibly from the time of the rebuilding of the south transept during Bishop Bancroft's restoration in the 1630s. However, this may well have replaced an earlier window which had decayed, and would have probably been a square headed window similar to that replaced in the south transept in the Victorian restoration. If the window is original it was presumably intended to provide additional light for the rood. The south porch was also added in this period and has benches on both sides. It was later converted into a vestry, probably in late Victorian times.[41] In addition, the large west window was added above the door which appears to point to the transition from the decorated to the perpendicular periods. Parker describes this window as 'a very singular one, of three lights, cinquefoiled, with quatrefoils in the head, and a transom across the springing of the arch'.[42] There are also some curious stone pilasters which possibly supported a gallery.

It is also possible that the chancel, which was traditionally the rector's responsibility, may perhaps have been lengthened to its present elongated proportions by the abbey at about this time: in the Treasurer's accounts of Abingdon Abbey for the year 1375-6 there is an entry under the heading

Above 3.4. South aisle windows (MC)
Below 3.5. South Porch with sundial (probably eighteenth-century). Henry Taunt (COS)

3.6. West window (MC)

3.7. Small north aisle window (MC)

'Expense in novo opre' which runs 'in petris emptis ibidem xli. ix s. iii d., unde ls., super cancellam des Cudd[esdon].'[43] The stone used was from the quarry at Wheatley, which also supplied stone for the Abbey.[44] Also at about this time the trefoil headed single lights in the clerestory were added, as was the large window in the north wall of the north transept, which retains a few fragments of painted medieval glass.[45]

Perhaps the most puzzling feature of the church is the small trefoil headed window with a transom dividing it from a small square low side window at the north-east end of the north aisle. The date and purpose of this window have been a matter of some debate. Following Parker, Davies rather implausibly speculates that it might have been a 'lychnoscope' so that people outside the church could watch the action at the altar. Parker also wrote that 'it opens at present into a small vestry, but this is a modern arrangement, it is probable that there was orig-inally an altar close to it'.[46] However, this seems unlikely since, as Parker himself notes, these were usually found only in chancels, and are normally to be found inside churches (as, for instance, at Great Haseley). Cuddesdon's substantial stair turret would

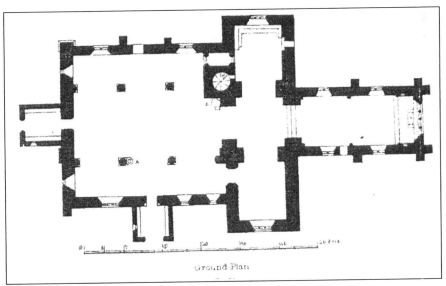

Ground Plan

3.8. Parker's 1846 Plan showing closed-off Room from Parker's *Guide*

have obliterated the view to the high altar, which presumably explains Parker's positing of another altar. The plan in Parker's guide indicates that the passage between the aisle and north transept was closed at either end to form a vestry, and the churchwardens' accounts record expenditure of £4 12s. 4d. on glass and joinery in 1828 for a 'new room', which might indicate that the window was perhaps of this late period.[47] There may well have been an earlier wall closing off the east end of the aisle, perhaps added in the seventeenth century for strength: this might explain the puzzling exterior, which seems to indicate that the west wall of the transept was moved at some point. Above and below the window is rough stone infill but with faced stone on each side. This, together with a higher roof line on the west side of the transept may indicate that the transept originally extended further west. However, these may simply be evidence of the constant repairs which had to be made to the church.

Late Medieval Church Life

There is very little evidence of church life and ministry in Cuddesdon from the thirteenth to the fifteenth centuries. All that survives are a few names of vicars and other ministers, but with very little additional information. Shortly after his appointment as vicar in 1239, Richard was required to appear in 1245 before the Bishop on the feast of St Michael. In 1249 Mr Thomas de Haregrafe, a deacon, was presented by John, Abbot of Abingdon and the

Convent to the vicarage.[48] In 1252, Johannes de Gnatteshall ('capellanus') was appointed vicar.[49] On 5 June 1270 Roger de Sutton was instituted vicar at Stow Park.[50] There is then complete silence for the fourteenth century. By the fifteenth century, however, it would appear that the vicars of Cuddesdon had become non-resident. In January 1407/8, for instance, during the episcopate of Philip Repingdon, Bishop of Lincoln, William Barrow was given permission to hold Cuddesdon in plurality with the rectory of Tackley, and to pronounce absolution in both places.[51] Shortly afterwards there was some attempt made to locate a centre of worship nearer the growing centre of population in Wheatley, which became a separate chapelry at least as early as 1427 and was ministered to by a number of chaplains or curates in the parish of Cuddesdon. In 1523 it was noted that a friar celebrated mass in the Wheatley chapel on festivals for a stipend of 40s. annually paid by the parishioners.[52]

John Hortope BCL was vicar of Cuddesdon in the latter part of the fifteenth century, his name occurring in relation to a dispute over the execution of his will in an undated deed in Snappe's formulary among the Bridgewater deeds dated between 1460 and 1497, most probably about the year 1490.[53] Later in the fifteenth century, John Estmondi (Edmund) MA, 'perpetual vicar of the parish church of Cuddesdon', was granted permission to hold Cuddesdon in plurality on 16 November 1497.[54] In 1516 Stephen Braudryb (Brawdribe) was granted a licence of non-residence by Bishop William Atwater,[55] and a few years later in 1520 the diocesan visitation noted that the vicar was non-resident.[56] In 1526 the subsidy collected in the diocese of Lincoln gives the name of Mag. Ricardus Stok' (Richard Stoke MA) as vicar. He was probably non-resident, and out of his income from the vicarage, which had increased to £16 13s. 4d.,[57] he paid £6 to a curate in Wheatley (Dom. Robertus Farnylle for the first part of the year, and Mag. Johannes Wayte, for the second part) as well as a further £6 13s. 6d. to Stephen Brawderibe, who was described as a 'pensioned vicar'.[58] Stoke was a prominent fellow of Magdalen who became president from 1507-10 and again from 1514-15, contesting the College presidency one more time in 1527.[59] He was also Rector of Great and Little Loughton, Bucks, and was still non-resident from Cuddesdon as late as 1540. It was also noted that he was disregarding the royal ordinance to distribute a fortieth of his benefice to the poor.[60]

The rebuilding of the Chancel

Perhaps as a result of this non-residence and changing demography, the church building at Cuddesdon seems to have been in a state of disrepair by the sixteenth century: in the 1520 diocesan visitation during Bishop Atwater's particularly active episcopate the chancel was noted as being in ruins ('ruinosus'), and it was reported that vestments and surplices were lacking.[61] Given that the abbey as rector was responsible for the repair of the chancel, this might explain the grand scheme for rebuilding shortly before the dissolution.

The original plan was possibly to have been to build aisles on to each side of the chancel, presumably similar to those of the nave. These may have connected with the Norman semi-pierced east walls in both the north and south transept with their round arches. The masonry may perhaps have been cut through to provide access on the completion of the aisles. Further evidence for the intended aisles is given by the pierced walls in the chancel itself (which might provide further evidence of the method of construction of the nave aisles), and which seem to have been built without windows. Parker remarked that the arches 'appear to have been made in the prospect of aisles being added, but are not carried through the whole thickness of the walls'.[62] Given that the arches are almost certainly part of the

3.9. Semi-pierced arch in south transept with modern altar (MC)

Left 3.10. Aumbry (MC)
Right 3.11. Piscina (MC)

original church this is highly unlikely, although it is possible that they would have been pierced if the chancel aisles had been added. The visitors from the Oxford Architectural Society in 1844, however, thought that the arches 'must have been built for ornament', although the absence of original windows makes this highly implausible.[63] There is also a fine perpendicular priest's doorway on the south side, which, with the east window, were 'the best parts of the design'.[64] The door was rather clumsily blocked up in the Victorian restoration (and was also obscured inside by the chancel furnishings). Had the work on the chancel been completed, Cuddesdon would have been a very grand church indeed. However, it is likely that the dissolution of the monasteries brought an abrupt halt to the rebuilding of the chancel. In 1846 Parker described two 'rude openings, with pointed arches, in the usual place of piscina and locker':[65] this roughness may well indicate a rapid cessation of work which may possibly have been patched up quickly. Similarly he noted 'two clumsy windows' on each side of the Chancel which were added later, and which again point to an abrupt halt to the building.[66]

In 1526 there was an attempt to grant the manor of Cuddesdon to Cardinal Wolsey's new College in Oxford (which became Christ Church) which had been built on the site of S. Frideswide's priory.[67] However, it seems

unlikely that this was successful, since as late as 1537, shortly before the dissolution, the Abbot of Abingdon offered a Mr Aisheton the farm of Cuddesdon
for £29 14s. 4d. rent per year. This rent from the demesne farm was supple-
mented by another £14 5s. 0d from other tenants.[68] Such sums would
certainly have been sufficient for the completion of the rebuilding of the
chancel. Indeed Abingdon Abbey remained an immensely wealthy institution: at the time of the dissolution on 29 May 1537 its annual income stood
at £1876 10s. 9d., a huge sum for those days. A further example of the revival
of the church in the 1520s and 30s is the bequest of William Bayley who in
1529 left 'his beste goode' as mortuary, bequeathing 20d. 'to buy a pursse to
carry the blessed sacrament to visitacions within the parish'.[69] At the 1539
valuation the Abbey's estates in the parish of Cuddesdon were worth about
£60.[70]

With the dissolution of the great Abbey of Abingdon, which had proved
so central to the history of Cuddesdon for at least five hundred years, a new
chapter of history begins: without the Abbey's protection, the future of the
Church in Cuddesdon was far from secure.

NOTES

1   Barlow, *The English Church, 1000-1066*, p. 200.
2   See Pounds, *A History of the English Parish*, ch. 1 and Barlow, *The English Church,
     1000-1066*, pp. 199-206.
3   Snape, *English Monastic Finances*, p. 77.
4   Barlow, *The English Church, 1066-1154*, p. 50. On this, see R. H. Snape, *English
     Monastic Finances in the Later Middle Ages*, Cambridge: Cambridge University Press,
     1926, pp. 76-91.
5   Snape, *English Monastic Finances*, p. 81.
6   H. E. Salter (ed.), *Oseney Abbey Cartulary*, iv, Oxford: Oxford Historical Society, 97,
     1934, p. 375.
7   C. R. Cheney, *From Becket to Langton*, Manchester: Manchester University Press,
     1956, p. 81.
8   A parallel example is that Master Elias who obtained a papal mandate from
     Celestine III for nomination to the Abingdon living of Chieveley in 1199. See
     Cheney, *From Becket to Langton*, p. 178.
9   On the history of the establishment of vicarages in Oxfordshire, see *VCH*, ii, pp. 10-
     12. It would appear that the earliest date from the time of St Hugh (1186-1200), and
     more were established during the episcopate of Hugh Wells (1209-35). Five marks
     seems to have been the minimum stipend during this time. A mark was worth 13*s*
     4*d*.
10   John became Cardinal Deacon of SS. Cosmas and Damian in the fourth promo-
     tion of Innocent III after 30 May 1205. He was succeeded in 1216. Konrad Eubel,
     Hierarchia Catholica medii aevi, Monasterii Sumptibus et typis Librariae
     Regensbergianae, 1898-1910, i, p. 4.
11   C. R. and M. G. Cheney (eds.), *Letters of Innocent III*, p. 49 (no. 296).

12   C. R. and M. G. Cheney (eds.), *Letters of Innocent III*, p. 133 (no. 804).

13   C. R. and M. G. Cheney (eds.), *Letters of Innocent III*, p. 136.

14   *CC*, p. 77.

15   For the papal mandate of 2 January 1209 see C. R. and M. G. Cheney (eds.), *Letters of Innocent III*, no. 820.

16   Cheney, *From Becket to Langton*, p. 80. There is some confusion about this John, since he was earlier involved in a dispute in 1203 over the rights to 'Gotesdon' church. This cannot have been Cuddesdon, since the rectory was at the time in the hands of the other John. Cheney surmises that it was Little Gaddesdon in Herts (p. 196). Joannes de Columna is mentioned in Eubel (i, p. 4) as cardinal of S. Praxedis from 15 March 1212 to his death on 17 Jan 1244/5.

17   For the early perpetual vicarages in the diocese of Lincoln, see Cheney, *From Becket to Langton*, pp. 182-5.

18   *CC*, pp. 85-6. The deed is calendared in W. H. Bliss et al, (eds), *Calendar of entries in the Papal Registers relating to Great Britain and Ireland (1198-1409)*, 4 vols, London: HMSO, 1893-1902, i, p. 129. See also p. 126 for a similar indult dated April 1231 for the appropriation of Cuddesdon to the uses of hospitality. Cf. i, 132 of 12 March 1233.

19   *CC*, p. 88.

20   Pounds, *A History of the English Parish*, p. 53; Snape, *English Monastic Finances*, p. 81.

21   *CC*, p. 88.

22   Bliss (ed.), *Cal. pap. lett.*, i., 132.

23   *CC*, p. 87.

24   *CC*, p. 88.

25   *CC*, p. 89. Cf. F. N. Davis (ed.) *Rotuli Roberti Grosseteste*, London: Canterbury and York Society, 10, 1913, p. 454. Also published as *Rotuli Roberti Grosseteste and Henry of Lexington*, (Lincoln Record Society 11), 1914, pp. 454-5. Cf. *VCH*, ii, p. 11. Fulwell was established in 1238.

26   Lambrick, 'Abingdon Abbey Administration', p. 159. For the wealth of the monastery see also *HEA*, p. lxxxv.

27   *CC*, p. 142.

28   William E. Lunt (ed.), *Valuation of Norwich*, Oxford: Clarendon Press, 1926, p. 306. On the economics of the medieval church, see Pounds, *A History of the English Parish*, pp. 201-14.

29   *Taxatio Ecclesiastica*, p. 30. The tithes from other lands in Cuddesdon yielded £9 19*s*. 8*d*. and from animals and fruit, £1 4*s*. 6*d*.

30   *Nonarum inquisitiones in Curia scaccarii: temp. regis Edwardi iii*, London: Record Commission, 1807, p. 133.

31   *LC*, pp. 91-2. See *Rotuli Roberti Grosseteste*, pp. 454-5. This is reckoned in *VCH*, v, as £13 6*s*. 8*d*.

32   *Rotuli Roberti Grosseteste and Henry of Lexington*, (LRS 11), 1914, p. 463.

33   *Valuation of Norwich*, p. 307.

34   *Taxatio Ecclesiastica* p. 30.

35   *CC*, p. 90. The average income of a vicar in the diocese of Lincoln was about one-third of the total income of the church (Snape, *English Monastic Finances*, p. 81).

36   Parker, *Guide*, p. 291.

37   *Oxford Architectural Society* NS III (1878), 'Walks and Excursions', Lent Term 1878, pp. 305-6. Italics in original

38   Parker, *Guide*, p. 292. See also the note on rood lofts in the *Archaeological Journal* 67 (1910), p. 184.

39   Parker, *Guide*, p. 292.

40   Parker, *Guide*, p. 292.

41   It was used as a vestry in 1887. See W. M. G. Ducat, *The Story of Cuddesdon Parish Church. A Sermon*, Preached in the Parish Church, 13 November 1887, (privately printed), Oxford, 1887

42   Parker, *Guide*, p. 292

43   R. E. G. Kirk (ed.), *Accounts of the Obedientiars of Abingdon Abbey*, pp. 289ff.

44   *VCH*, v, p. 112.

45   Parker, *Guide*, p. 292.

46   Parker, *Guide*, p. 293.

47   ORO MS DD Par Cuddesdon b. 5 fol 24.

48   *Rotuli Roberti Grosseteste and Henry of Lexington*, (LRS 11), 1914, p. 493.

49   *Rotuli Roberti Grosseteste and Henry of Lexington*, (LRS 11), 1914, p. 501.

50   F. N. Davis (ed.), *Rotuli Ricardi Gravesend*, (LRS 20), 1925, p. 222; cf. Parker p. 297.

51   Margaret Archer (ed.), *Register of Bp. Philip Repingdon, 1405-1419*, i, LRS 57 (1962), pp. 108-9.

52   *VCH*, ii, pp. 14-15; *VCH*, v, p. 114.

53   H. E. Salter (ed.), *Snappe's Formulary and Other Records*, Oxford: OHS 80, 1924, p. 260.

54   Anne P. Fuller (ed.), *Calendar of Papal Registers Relating to Great Britain and Ireland*, Dublin: Irish Stationery Office, 1986, xvi, p. 546 (no. 802).

55   Margaret Bowker (ed.), *An Episcopal Court Book for the Diocese of Lincoln: 1514-1520*, LRS 61 (1967), p. 18.

56   A. Hamilton Thompson (ed.), *Visitations in the Diocese of Lincoln*, 1517-31, i, LRS (33), 1940, p. 137.

57   At the dissolution the value had risen slightly to £17 11s. 0d. (*Valor Ecclesiastias Henry VIII*, London, 1802, ii, p. 172).

58   H. E. Salter (ed.), *A Subsidy Collected in the Diocese of Lincoln in 1526*, ORS 63 (1909), p. 257.

59   William Dunn Macray, *A Register of the Members of St Mary Magdalen College, Oxford*, i, London: Froude, 1894, esp. pp. 140-1.

60   *VCH*, v, p. 104. James Gairdner and R.H. Brodie (eds.), *Letters and Papers of Henry VIII*, London: HMSO, 1894, xiv (1), p. 604.

61   *Visitations in the Diocese of Lincoln*, 1517-31, i., p. 137. See also Margaret Bowker, *The Secular Clergy in the Diocese of Lincoln, 1495-1520*, Cambridge: Cambridge University Press, 1968.

62   Parker, *Guide*, p. 293.

63   *Oxford Architectural Society Meeting*, 1 May 1844, p. 5f.

64   Parker, *Guide*, p. 292.

65   Parker, *Guide*, p. 293.

66   Parker, *Guide*, p. 293. These windows were replaced by more fitting designs during the first Victorian restoration.

67   J. S. Brewer (ed), *Letters and Papers of Henry VIII*, London: HMSO, 1870, iv (1), pp. 848-9, p. 587.

68   J. S. Brewer (ed), *Letters and Papers of Henry VIII*, London: HMSO, 1890, xii (1), p. 556. Sir William Dugdale, *Monasticon Anglicanum*, London: Longman, 1817, i, 529.

69   *VCH*, v, p. 106.

70   Dugdale records that the manor of Cuddesdon was valued at £29 13s 4d. Other land from Cuddesdon was valued at £14 5s; Denton was valued at £10 9s. 8d. and

Wheatley £9 14s. The mill yielded £5, La Vente farm in Forest Hill, £4 6s. 8d., tithes in Wheatley £6 6s 8d. and from the portion of the parish in Holton, 6s. 8d. Cf. Parker, *Guide*, p. 298.

Chapter Four

Cuddesdon in the Aftermath of the Reformation

The Dissolution of Abingdon Abbey

After the dissolution of Abingdon Abbey things changed rapidly in Cuddesdon.[1] Throughout the country there was a wholesale redistribution of ecclesiastical land and benefices. Cuddesdon rectory reverted to the Crown, and the tithes were granted in 1539 to Sir John Brome of Holton.[2] Land in Cuddesdon was also granted to John Sheriff of Essex.[3] The Reformation also brought with it the keeping of parish records: the baptismal records of Cuddesdon parish begin in 1541 when there were twelve baptisms. In the following year, when burial records began, there were twenty-one burials. The advowson was exercised by a clerk named John Broke who instituted John Robins to the living 'under the Abbot and Convent of Abingdon Monastery' on 15 December 1546 (even though the abbey had been dissolved). At about this time the manor was in the hands of the Crown and being farmed by John Egerley, royal bailiff of the 'Cuddesdon lordship',[4] but was granted in 1545 to Browne Edmunds.[5] The advowson of Cuddesdon was excluded from a subsequent grant of the manor made in 1558.[6] Later in Elizabeth's reign Richard Nevill secured a 21-year lease of all buildings, orchard, glebe and tithes for £17 13s. 4d.[7] In addition, the great tithes of Wheatley were appropriated by the Crown but separated from those of Cuddesdon. These passed through a number of hands until the nineteenth century.[8]

It is impossible to know whether there was much opposition to the Reformation in Cuddesdon, although Oxfordshire appears to have accepted the religious changes with relative calmness. Nevertheless there was an immediate physical impact of the acts of redistribution following the reformation on the church building: without the abbey to care for its fabric Cuddesdon church fell rapidly into disrepair in the later years of the sixteenth century. The exposed south-westerly position meant that the stonework again proved to be a drain on diminishing resources. At an archdeacon's court of October 1584, the 'guardians' of Cuddesdon, Robert Simes and John Munt, were ordered to repair the church.[9] The vicar at the time was Ralph Marler who had served from 1573/4.[10]

Religious practice also changed rapidly:[11] the differences between the inventories of 28 July 1552 (the year of the second Book of Common Prayer) and the following year are striking. In the former inventory 'a cope of crimosin velvet, 2 copes of yellow satten, and one old cope and a payre of vestiments in red' are listed, along with another four sets of vestiments, as well as '3 paynted clothes for the sepulchre'. Yet by 17 May 1553 there is no mention of any of these: all that was left of the vestiments were three surplices and two rochets.[12] One chalice had also been lost in this period. In some villages (as, for instance, at Pyrton) some church silver was apparently stolen, although there is no evidence for this at Cuddesdon.[13] Indeed, despite the loss of some of its treasures, Cuddesdon retained more of its possessions than many other local churches.

It would seem that Cuddesdon was no exception to the general pattern of reformation in Edwardian England: most of the trappings of the medieval cult were removed with great haste. Along with the vestiments and silver, the rood screen was also probably removed in this period. In the present building there is very little remaining of the medieval interior decoration of the church, although there are still slight traces of medieval painting around the small east window of the north transept. What is left comprises red petals with brown

4.1. Remains of Medieval Painting in North Transept (MC)

stems and green intertwining. In 1949, when the transept was re-ordered, more was uncovered – imposed over the flower and leaf work were two large angels with spreading wings, one on each side of the arch. Unfortunately these were too fragile to be left uncovered.

The Foundation of the Diocese of Oxford

What later proved to be the most significant event of these years for Cuddesdon was Henry VIII's foundation of the new diocese of Oxford in 1542 with the last Abbot of Oseney and suffragan Bishop of Rheon, Robert King, as its first bishop.[14] This episcopal reorganisation, which seems to have been a long-established idea in the king's mind, perhaps dating back to 1528 when Wolsey had applied for the suppression of twenty-one monasteries to endow new dioceses, made a huge impact on the village and church in Cuddesdon. Indeed it was the foundation of the diocese of Oxford that marks out Cuddesdon from so many similar villages. Without the Bishops of Oxford, Cuddesdon would have followed the pattern of many hundreds of similar parish churches into the next centuries. The church would no doubt have survived as an impressive building with interesting though not outstanding architectural features. Yet because of the Bishops of Oxford it was destined for a history which brought it to the forefront, first of the new diocese of Oxford and then of the whole of the Church of England.

The early years of the diocese of Oxford, however, were far from auspicious. After the death of Robert King in 1557 the see was unoccupied for thirty years apart from a brief period when the aged Hugh Curwen, who had been Archbishop of Dublin, lived out his last year as Bishop of Oxford between 1567 and 1568. Since there was no provision for an episcopal residence Curwen lived in Swinbrook near Burford, where, 'very decrepid, broken with old age and many state affairs,' he died and was buried in the Parish Church.[15] The original building intended for the palace (part of the medieval Gloucester Hall) had reverted to the Crown in the reign of Edward VI and had since been taken over by Worcester College. Bishop King, it seems, had lived in the building now occupied by the Roman Catholic Chaplaincy in Rose Place opposite Christ Church. King's arms occur several times on the moulding of the ground floor ceiling.[16] Although the Cathedral Chapter had been sufficiently endowed during Edward's reign by Letters Patent, this was not the case for the see. Political expediency meant that lands earmarked for the bishop's endowment were diverted to the Crown for interests of state in the early years of the reign of Elizabeth: Browne Willis estimated that £193 16s. 9½d. was taken away from the Edwardian endowment during this period.[17] It was clear that if the see was going to survive the question of a suitable endowment would have to be settled urgently.

To this end various impropriations[18] were exchanged for the estates which had been taken from the see, the Crown again making use of the Edwardian Letters Patent. It was as part of this exchange that the rectory of Cuddesdon, still at £17 13s. 4d. was granted to the see. The advowson of Cuddesdon vicarage was also attached to the see in 1589, Cuddesdon thereby becoming one of only twelve benefices to which the Bishop of Oxford had the right of presentation. Other episcopal impropriations were those of Stanton Harcourt, Culham, Banbury, Cropredy, Burford with Fulbrook, and Ambrosden. Browne Willis estimated the total value to be £201 11s. 6d.[19] These endowments meant that the see was able to be filled after a period of twenty-one years, John Underhill, chaplain to Elizabeth, becoming bishop in 1589. His tenure lasted less than three years and he died in May 1592 'in much discontent and poverty'.[20] He does not seem to have been very active in his brief tenure of the see: there are no records of any ordinations in his time; indeed there are no records of him having come into the diocese at all.[21] The principal reason for the Bishop's inactivity and poverty, it would seem, was that the level of his endowments still remained insufficient.

Cuddesdon provides a good example of the levels of confiscation and redistribution of ecclesiastical revenue in the years following the dissolution of the monasteries: most of the land in the village had been transferred to the Gardiner family, with only about one ninth of the whole being given to the bishop. After John Underhill's death the see remained vacant for a further twelve years and again there was a decline in the income of the diocese. During vacancies the episcopal revenues reverted to the Crown and could be used for non-ecclesiastical purposes. There was little sense of urgency on the part of the Crown to appoint a successor. Wood noted that by 1603 'the patrimony of the bishopric' was 'much dilapidated and made a prey (for the most part) to Robert, Earl of Essex, to whom it proved miserably fatal'.[22] During the periods when there was no bishop most of the episcopal duties were undertaken by the archdeacons, Walter Wright (1543-61), John Kennall (1561-92) and John Drury (1592-1614).[23] It was only with the appointment of John Bridges in 1604, that, according to one contemporary writer, the see of Oxford was prevented from drowning 'in a sea of oblivion'.[24] Bridges lived 'for the most part in hired houses in the county' including one at Marsh Baldon, where he died on 25 March 1618 and where he was buried in the chancel of the church.[25]

With the gradual improvement of the state of the diocese in the early years of the seventeenth century, it would seem that some efforts were made to

General View from the South-west.

4.2. The Church in 1846 before restoration showing pinnacles from Parker's *Guide*

repair and improve the bishop's own churches including Cuddesdon. Edmund Underhill, who had taken his BA at Lincoln College in 1590, was inducted as vicar in 1606 on the presentation of the Bishop. During his time as incumbent much building and repair work was undertaken: at some point in the early Stuart years the tower was repaired and its upper part was rebuilt, possibly for the installation of new bells. The pinnacles and parapet,[26] about which Alfred Pott complained in 1848, were probably also added at this time. Given the dates of the bells this might mean a slightly earlier date than the 1630 suggested by Jennifer Sherwood.[27] It was also at this time that the Norman groin was removed and replaced with a wooden ringing chamber. The corbels, however, were left and the slope can be clearly seen in Parker's drawings of 1846.[28] There are remains of a door high in the south wall of the north transept against the tower which served as an entrance to the belfry for the hoisting of the bells. A peal of 4 bells and a 'little' (presumably a sanctus) bell and 2 handbells were listed in the 1552 inventory.[29] The sanctus bell was not included in the following year. These earlier bells were recast or replaced

4.3. Belfry today (MC)

as part of the general improvement made during Bridges' episcopate: the no. 2 bell is dated 1617 (6 cwt) and is tuned to C. Number 3 is also dated 1617 (7 cwt) and tuned to Bb. No. 4 is tuned to A (8 cwt). All three were made by Henry Knight.[30]

The earliest monuments in the church also date from these years. Wood mentioned a brass on the south aisle wall to George Barston of Chippinghurst who died in 1607. Another, located originally on the north side of the chancel and now on the west wall of the north transept, also dates from these years: it commemorates James King (d. 27 July 1620), gentleman, citizen and cloth-maker and sometime Master of the Clothmaker's Company and a former student of Brasenose.[31]

Cuddesdon, Wheatley and Recusancy

In 1630 there was a careful survey of Cuddesdon Church (which may possibly have been connected with the idea of using Cuddesdon as an epis-copal residence). The seating was noted as being in great decay.[32] Part of the reason for this was the reluctance of Wheatley parishioners to contribute to the repairs of the parish church. At the dissolution the small tithes of Wheatley had been retained by the Vicar of Cuddesdon, which meant that the village was still unable to finance a priest of its own. There was evidently some pressure for change from the population of Wheatley, led by Abraham Archdale of Wheatley Manor.[33] The Archdales had moved to Wheatley from

Right 4.4. James King Monument (MC)
Below 4.5. Wheatley Manor (1601). Home of the Archdales (COS)

Denton in 1568, Abraham inheriting the house on the death of his father, Richard in 1577. Richard, who had remained sympathetic to the old religion, had asked 'to be buried in the midst of the cross-way in Cuddesdon Church where the Crucifix did stand and I trust in God shall stand again'.[34] Abraham's mother, Mary, and elder brother, John (who had probably made over the house to the bachelor, Abraham), were returned as recusants (Roman Catholics) in 1577.

There had been a dispute between Cuddesdon and Wheatley from at least as early as 1628 when the vicar of Cuddesdon produced 'eight good reasons

why Wheatley Chapel should not be consecrated a church in its own right'.[35] Such an action would, he claimed, have led to a loss of revenue for Cuddesdon, as well as the loss of the vicar's right to nominate a 'reader' for Wheatley.[36] By the early 1600s Wheatley had grown in size and was far larger than Cuddesdon: in 1612 it had more than 283 communicants, whereas Cuddesdon (in 1665) had only nine substantial farmers paying hearth tax. In 1629 Wheatley defended its right to elect a churchwarden to its (unconsecrated) chapel 'without any interposing meddling or challenging any right or interest in the said election by the Vicar of Cuddesdon ... or by the parishioners ... of Cuddesdon or Denton.' Again this was opposed by the vicar of Cuddesdon with a protest against 'the inconveniences which are likely to grow to the church, the vicar and inhabitants ... by the consecration of the chapel of Wheatley without saving and reserving of the ancient right, immunities, usages and customs due to the said church and vicar'.[37]

The Archdeacon's inspection of Cuddesdon early in 1630 noted that 'The seats in the body of the church are in great decay and the body of the said church also' and required the churchwardens or 'guardians of Cuddesdon', William Rider, Fromain Hanley and John Saunders to appear before an Ecclesiastical Court on 30 April 1630 in Oxford to explain themselves. This provoked much hostility from the Wheatley parishioners. The Court Books of the Registry of the Bishop of Oxford noted that

> The inhabitants in Wheatley being part of this Parish refuse to contribute toward the reparation of the said seats. That is the reason they are not repaired for the inhabitants of Wheatley say they are not bound to repair those seats except they may have seats appointed them in the Church. It was decided that the inhabitants of Cuddesdon, Denton and Chippinghurst do repair those seats and in case the parish do build seats for the inhabitants of Wheatley in Cuddesdon Church, then the inhabitants of Wheatley to contribute thereto. And the church wardens are enjoined to see those seats and the ruins of the church now in decay, to be repaired by Bartholomews day next.[38] And to certify the [next ?] day thereof following.[39]

The pews were presumably repaired (if reluctantly) after this time, and it is also quite likely that a west gallery was added to provide additional seating.

Some of the seats have plain square ends, some have poppy heads, somewhat rudely carved in the shape of fleurs-de-lys. A simple wooden screen in front of the crossing arch, which can be clearly made out in the drawing in the *Gentleman's Magazine* of 1821, could well have been added in this period. It was probably also in this period that the current nave roof was constructed.

Above
4.6. Carvings on pews (MC)
Left
4.7. West Door showing crossing screen from *Gentleman's Magazine* xci (1821), pp. 201-2

It was stripped of the old tile roofing and re-covered in lead sheets. The pitch was lowered considerably leaving the old line visible on the west tower wall; the whole of the wall at the west end of the nave which carried the original roof was also left standing.[40]

It was this controversy over the pews that probably led to Abraham Archdale cancelling a legacy of £40 he had promised to Cuddesdon Church, and instead giving £100 to the poor of Wheatley, £10 to Oxford University, £5 to the poor of St Martin's, Oxford, and £3 to the poor of Cuddesdon. He also cancelled his intention of being buried near his mother at Cuddesdon in favour of burial at Wheatley. He left the staggering sum of £300 for a monument and made a request to the Bishop of Oxford 'to consecrate the said chapel and ground adjoining for a place of burial'.[41] No records exist of any Archdale monument in Wheatley chapel.

There was some further conflict in these years involving recusants within the ancient parish of Cuddesdon. Although never more than a handful, some, like the Archdales, were notable landowners. In 1607 Maria Horseman, who lived at Wheatley in the parish from 1603-30, was fined for non-attendance at church. Her mother Elizabeth, was widow of Paul Horseman, a JP from Great Haseley and was perhaps Archdale's sister. She was repeatedly fined for non-attendance at church but acquired a certain notoriety after her death on 31 December 1630. During the night of 5 January 1630/1, though excommunicated, she received a clandestine burial under the communion table of Holton church,[42] perhaps by the Rector, Bartholomew Price, who, according to the Inquiry, had promised 'in her lifetime that he would bury her when she was dead'.[43] She had also received nursing care from Mary Wicker, wife of the curate of Wheatley.

Mrs Horseman's body was apparently moved from her garden (where she had been placed because her body had started to smell) to the church under cover of darkness.[44] This led to a sensational case in the Bishop's Court since nobody, including the landlord of the White Hart, could be found to bear witness against the perpetrators.[45] Numbers of Catholics seem to have declined in later years. Whereas in 1624 there were three recusants living in the parish of Cuddesdon, by 1768 there were only two aged 'papists' who were described as 'quite inoffensive' and in the 1771 visitation the only 'papist' returned was a 'poor gardener'.[46] At the 1778 visitation there were no papists, Presbyterians, Independents or Anabaptists, and in 1780 there were no papists.[47]

NOTES

1   *VCH*, ii, p. 30. On the Reformation in the Diocese of Lincoln, see Margaret Bowker, *The Henrician Reformation in the Diocese of Lincoln under John Longland, 1521-1547*, Cambridge: Cambridge University Press, 1981. On the Reformation in Cuddesdon and the surrounding area see John Fox, *The Reformation in the Villages*, Wheatley: Privately Printed, 1996.

2   On the Bromes, see Fox, *The Reformation*, pp. 21-5.

3   James Gairdner and R.H. Brodie (eds), *Letters and Papers of Henry VIII*, xiv (1), p. 604.

4   *VCH*, v, p. 102.

5   ORO ODP c. 2148 f. 1.

6   For the history of the manor after the dissolution, see *VCH*, v, pp. 101-2.

7   *VCH*, v, p. 104.

8   *VCH*, v, p. 114.

9   E. R. Brinkworth (ed.), *The Archdeacon's court: Liber actorum, 1584*, ORS 23, 1942, (October 1584), i, p. 16.

10   ORO Archd. Oxon e.11, p. 116 (1585).

11   For other local examples of the dissolution of the medieval cult, see *VCH*, ii, p. 34.

12   Rose Graham (ed.), *The Edwardian Inventories for Oxfordshire*, ORS 1, 1919, pp. 65, 127.

13   *VCH*, ii, p. 34. Pyrton has particularly good records for the period: the Books of Homilies and the King's Injunctions were bought in 1547. In the same year all rents for the maintenance of lights were surrendered, supposedly for the maintenance of the poor.

14   See *VCH*, ii, pp. 29, 31-2.

15   Anthony à Wood, *Athenae Oxonienses*, (ed. P. Bliss), London: Rivington, 1815, ii, p. 804. Details of the original endowment, which amounted to £341 18s 9d., are included in Browne Willis, *A Survey of the Cathedrals*, London: R. Gosling, 1730, iii, p. 402. For the early history of the diocese see pp. 402-74.

16   Edward Marshall, *Diocesan Histories: Oxford*, London: SPCK, 1882, p. 97.

17   Browne Willis, *Survey*, iii, p. 417.

18   This is equivalent to the medieval system of appropriation of ecclesiastical revenues to religious houses, but when the rectory is given to a lay impropriator (e.g. an Oxford or Cambridge College or a private individual). It was widely regarded as simply another tax to be paid.

19   Browne Willis, *Survey*, iii, p.417; see also Marshall, *Oxford*, p.119. On this, see Christopher Hill, *Economic Problems of the Church from Whitgift to the Long Parliament*, Oxford: Clarendon Press, 1956, pp. 8-9, 234-6.

20   Wood, *Athenae Oxonienses*, ii, p. 830.

21   Marshall, *Oxford*, p. 115.

22   Wood, *Athenae Oxonienses*, ii, col. 831. Cf. Marshall, *Oxford*, p. 118.

23   *VCH*, ii, p. 40.

24   Sir J. Harrington, cited in Marshall, *Oxford*, p. 118. Cf. Browne Willis, *Survey*, p. 432.

25   Wood, *Athenae Oxonienses*, ii, pp. 893-4.

26   These can be clearly seen in Parker's picture (*Guide*, p. 289). Modest pinnacles remained until the 1960s.

27   Sherwood and Pevsner, *Oxfordshire*, p. 562.

28   See above Plate 2.4.

29   Rose Graham (ed.), *The Edwardian Inventories for Oxfordshire*, pp. 65, 127.

30   One of the other three of the present six bells was added in 1795 (the treble), a gift of the Bishop of Oxford (Edward Smallwell), tuned to D (5 cwt). At the time of Parker's 1846 guide there were seven bells, one of 1677, one of 1709 and 'a little one' of 1748 (p. 294). The *Gentleman's Magazine* XCI (May, 1821), mentions only six bells in 1821. Presumably some of these bells were recast when in 1863 two new bells were added (no. 5 tuned to G (9 cwt) and tenor tuned to F (14 cwt), both made by G. Mears and Co.). The seventeenth century oak bell frame was restored in 1949 by R. White and Sons, with new bell fittings added (Frederick Sharpe, *The Church Bells of Oxfordshire*, vol. 1 (Oxford: Oxfordshire Record Society, vol. 28, 1949), p. 108) and *Cuddesdon News*, April 1973.

31   F. N. Davis (ed.), *Parochial Collections made by Anthony à Wood, MA and Richard Rawlinson*, ORS 2, 1920, pp. 106-7. Monuments are described in Bod. MS Top. Oxon. b. 220, ff. 118-20. Cf. Parker, *Guide*, p. 293.

32   Bod. MS Top. Oxon. c. 56 f. 28. *VCH*, ii, p. 41 cites many other court cases from the same years.

33   *VCH*, v, pp. 110, 115. Abraham is incorrectly called Archibald on p. 115. See also John Fox, *Tanning-Barn to Church. The Dissenting Congregation of Wheatley over Two Hundred Years*, Wheatley, 1997, p. 9-10; Fox, *The Reformation in the Villages*, p. 20.

34   John Fox (ed.), *One More Millennium: The Story of Wheatley and Holton Park*, Wheatley: Wheatley 2000, 2000, p. 15.

35   *VCH*, v, p. 114.

36   Hassall, *Records of Wheatley*, p. 65.

37   Cited in Malcolm Oxley, 'Wheatley in the Valley. Cuddesdon on the Hill' in Blair Worden, *Stuart England*, London: Phaidon, 1986, pp. 250-1.

38   It is incidentally extremely unlikely that the repairs were made by a local craftsman named 'Bartholomew Day' as the *Victoria County History* states (*VCH*, v, p. 105).

39   Bod. MS Top Oxon c. 56 f. 28, (Second article, 30 April 1630).

40   Parker, *Guide*, p. 293.

41   Will cited in Fox, *The Reformation*, p. 34.

42   The Bromes, who held Holton Manor, were frequently under suspicion of Recusancy.

43   Fox, *The Reformation*, p. 31.

44   Fox, *One More Millennium*, p. 18.

45   *VCH*, ii, p. 45.

46   *VCH*, v, pp. 98, 175.

47   ORO ODP c 432 f. 42.

Chapter Five

The Bishop Comes to Cuddesdon

The Building of the First Bishop's Palace

During most of Elizabeth's reign, when the bishopric remained vacant, the problem of the lack of an episcopal house was obviously not especially pressing. However, after the see had been re-occupied from 1604 with an adequate (though by no means generous) endowment, the need for accommodation became urgent, since it was hardly acceptable that bishops should be required to find their own housing. On his appointment as Bishop of Oxford on 23 August 1632 after Bishop Richard Corbet's translation to Norwich, John Bancroft (1574-1640),[1] nephew of the former Archbishop of Canterbury, Richard Bancroft (1544-1610), sought to remedy this deficiency once and for all. One of William Laud's projects was to improve the material conditions of the smaller bishoprics, and it was one of the conditions of Bancroft's appointment, which had been procured by Laud (who became Archbishop of Canterbury in 1633), that he should build a new house at his own expense.[2] Laud himself had even suggested Cuddesdon as a suitable location.[3] However, there remained the problem of financing the building. The first step in this process began in 1632 when the vicarage became vacant on the death of Edward Underhill. As patron of living, Bancroft, who had earlier been granted permission to hold cures to the value of £40, adopted the relatively unusual practice of presenting himself as vicar, holding the vicarage in commendam with the see, according to letters patent dated 2 June 1632, and using the income to help finance the building of a new palace.[4]

In many ways Cuddesdon proved an ideal site: it was on the bishop's own glebeland which meant that no land purchase was necessary,[5] and, perhaps more importantly, its exposed position meant that it did not suffer from Oxford's insanitary humidity, which put the city under constant threat from plague, typhus and cholera. Moving to a suitable hill outside Oxford was not an unusual practice for the Oxford elite. For instance, the parsonage house at neighbouring Garsington, where the rectory belonged to Trinity College, was often used in times of plague to house the President and fellows of the College.

The 1631 visitation had revealed the existing parsonage house to the north side of the church to be 'old and mean' and 'in a most ruinous condition'. Consequently it was imperative that a completely new house should be built. In the state papers confirming the annexation of the vicarage, there is a brief history of the building of the palace:

> Finding the vicarage house mean and ruinous [Bancroft] was desirous to build a house for the residence of himself and his successors on the glebe-land of the vicarage. For his encouragement therein the King bestowed on him 50 timber trees out of the forest of Shotover.[6]

According to a letter dated 18 March 1636 Bancroft also managed to obtain from the King a remittance of the sum of £343 7s. 11½d which would have been due from the first fruits (i.e. the first year's revenues accruing to a benefice which were payable as a form of tax to the crown).[7] The cost of the new palace was said to have been about £2,500.[8] The bishop also procured from the King an annual rent-charge of £100 secured on the forests of Shotover and Stowood.[9]

The palace, a 'fair place with a chapel in it', was completed by 1634[10] and in 1635 it accommodated Bancroft's mentor, Archbishop Laud and his vast retinue. Laud wrote in his diary on 2 September 1635:

> I was in attendance with the King at Woodstock, and went from there to Cudsden to see the house which Dr. John Bancroft, the Lord Bishop of Oxford, had there built to be a house for the Bishops of that See for ever; he having built that house at my persuasion.[11]

Laud stayed in Cuddesdon Palace, which he described as 'a faire house of stone', again on 4 September the following year on his way from London to Oxford to entertain the king in his role as Vice-Chancellor of the University. At that stage it could accommodate Laud's coach and six together with fifty horsemen, 'all his own servants'.[12]

The palace, a 'very good house',[13] is shown in a number of contemporary representations, including as a background to Bancroft's own portrait at University College.[14] It had its own chapel dedicated to St John the Evangelist, as well as an orchard and a surrounding garden.[15] The house was a substantial four storey building with four gables, together with an attached wing on the right-hand (presumably south) side. It is also interesting to note that at the same time as Bancroft was building the palace, another bishop was also established in the parish of Cuddesdon: in 1622 John Barston sold

5.1. Cuddesdon Palace in 1644 (Bod)

Denton manor house to William Piers (1580-1670), bishop successively of Peterborough (1630) and Bath and Wells (1632), who left the house to his son John, at his death.[16]

Not long after the completion of the Palace, the king gave permission to the Bishop to appropriate the vicarage (as well as the house) to the see.[17] The Royal Instructions explicitly mention that

> whereas John Bancroft doctor of divinity and Bishop of Oxford hath very worthily att his owne proper cost and charges, built a house for himselfe, and the Bishops of Oxford successively (by our leave and incouragement) upon the vicaridge of Cuddesden near Oxford, which vicaridge is in the patronage and guift of him and his successors. And whereas our further will and pleasure is, that the said house togeather with the vicaridge aforesaid, shall ever be held in commendum by the Bishopps of Oxford successively. That therefore the said bishop for the tyme being doe yearly give his particular accompt of his holding both the house and benefice aforesaid, to the end that wee and our successors may upon all occasions bee putt in minde of keeping that house and vicarage to the see of Oxford, att all tymes of change, when or howsoever that bishopricke shall become void.[18]

This annexation of the vicarage to the see caused some dissent in the diocese with the Archdeacon of Oxford, Barten Holyday complaining to Archbishop Laud, who in turn asked the archdeacon 'to shew cause why the Vicaridge of Cudesden should not be united to the Bishopric of Oxon for ever.'[19] The King confirmed the gift of Cuddesdon in 1637 stating that the bishop 'should appropriate the vicarage and Mansion House with the Glebe'.[20] The state papers issued in response to the controversy with Holyday note that the King

> on the bishop's petition now declares his pleasure that the said vicarage shall be perpetually united to the see of Oxford, or otherwise annexed as Archbishop Laud shall find cause, and that it shall pass in the Office of the Faculties, and be confirmed by the Great Seal, the Archbishop setting down a tax for the same, and providing for the service of the cure of the said parish. Having further considered the great mischiefs which have been bred in the ecclesiastical state, by the frequent appropriations of Churches in former times to monasteries and other ecclesiastical persons and places, the King directs that the Archbishop and Lord Keeper shall pass no such union without weighty cause first made known to his majesty, and sufficient provision made for serving the cure in parishes to be appropriated.[21]

These acts meant that the rectory and vicarage of Cuddesdon were permanently united in the hands of the bishop.[22] The King also commanded the bishop to limit the terms of leasing the rectory, a common practice which could impoverish future occupants.[23]

This unusual set of circumstances, with the bishop as both rector and vicar persisted until the nineteenth century. From the seventeenth century until the separation of the vicarage in 1852, Cuddesdon village was usually served by a curate or a chaplain paid for directly by the bishop. A second curate was responsible for the chapel at Wheatley. In 1635 two curates are mentioned in the Visitation documents, a Mr Whitaker and a Mr Parker, presumably one each for Cuddesdon and Wheatley.[24] In 1637 a charity was set up under the benefaction of John Child, who left the sum of £128 14s 3*d*. 'for the benefit of deserving and necessitous persons resident in the said Parish of Cuddesdon' and the five-hundred year lease of land at 18 Cornmarket, Thame at a ground rent of £4 per annum. The Child's charity was still being used to distribute money to deserving people as late as 1954 when £14 15s was paid to thirty-one poor of the parish. The rent was still being collected as late as 1973, but the freehold was eventually sold for £1000 in 1982. The money was invested, the modest income still benefiting the elderly of the parish.

The Civil War

Bishop Bancroft, however, did not have long to live in his new palace. As Anthony Wood noted, he was unable to cope with the political pressure of the times and died in February 1641 in Westminster, with no obvious signs of disease:

> In 1640 Long Parliament began, and proceeded with great vigour against the Bishops – he was possessed with so much fear – (having always been an enemy to the puritan) – that with little or no sickness – he surrendered up his last breath in his lodgings at Westminster. Afterwards his body was conveyed to Cuddesdon in the diocese of Oxford and was buried near to and under the south wall of the chancel of the church there, on the 12th day of February in 1640/1, leaving behind him the character, among the puritans of presbyterians then dominant, of a corrupt, unpreaching, Popish Prelate.[25]

His close association with Laud and Charles I meant that he was highly suspect among parliamentarians. Dr Barten Holyday later told Wood that Bancroft was buried in 'an isle of his owne building'. If this is the case it must refer to the south transept of the church which was rebuilt to Bancroft's plan and order in 1637, and which makes use of some earlier materials. Part of the north transept was also repaired during Bancroft's time.[26]

Bancroft's successor, Robert Skinner, who was translated from Bristol, retained the link with Cuddesdon. Shortly after his appointment, however, he was imprisoned in the Tower of London for eighteen weeks on a charge of high treason. After his release at the beginning of the Civil War he came to live at the palace with his wife, remaining until 1643 when he left to join the garrison in Oxford.[28] For the remainder of the Commonwealth period

5.2. Church in 1804 showing Bancroft's replacement window in south transept by C. Nattes (Bod) (MS Top. Oxon. b.3. fol. 37)[27]

Skinner lived at Launton near Bicester, where he had held the rectory in plurality since 1636.

Not long after Skinner had left the palace, it was burnt down towards the end of 1644 on the orders of Colonel William Legge,[29] commander of the Royal garrison.[30] This was primarily to prevent its use as a parliamentary barracks during the siege of Oxford. The River Thame, which forms a substantial section of the boundary of Cuddesdon parish, acted as a natural barrier between the opposing forces, and at one point a gate was erected on Wheatley bridge. Legge's act of arson seems to have been an astute move: during the Civil War, first parliamentarian (1644) and then Royalist troops (1646) were billeted elsewhere in Cuddesdon.[31] In 1643 the registers note the burial of two soldiers from Wheatley, and in the following year another three were buried from Denton.

Wood much regretted the burning: 'though with as much reason and more piety (as [Peter Heylin] observes) he might have garrisoned it for the King, and preserved the house. Being thus ruined, it lay so till Dr. John Fell became Bishop of Oxford.'[32] In 1652 the Parliamentary Commission sold the palace land and the chapel. So complete was the destruction that after the restoration there is no mention of the palace whatsoever in the hearth tax returns of 1665.[33]

Sir Thomas Gardiner, Recorder of London and Solicitor General to the King and a prominent royalist, had inherited Cuddesdon Manor shortly before the Civil War.[34] After his goods were seized by parliament in 1643, he ordered the burning of the Manor House, again to prevent its use by Parliamentarian forces. Gardiner himself was banished to Cuddesdon and was buried on 15 October 1652, reputedly in a vault under the high altar. The house was probably first built when the manor was leased by the abbey in 1421: it was a fifteenth-century building connected to the churchyard by steps, with its own 'chekkaer' and chapel.[35] The exact whereabouts of the Manor House are unknown, although it seems most likely that it occupied land to the south side of the church probably where Dove House now stands. It is interesting to note that Dove House contains evidence of burnt timber. In drawings in the Bodleian Library entitled 'Ruins at Cuddeston' by C. Nattes dated 1804 there are recognisable Tudor ruins just south of the churchyard. The Manor House was never rebuilt: the present house now called The Manor was until recently called Manor Farm House. The suggestion in the *Victoria County History* that this was built on the site of the Manor does not seem possible given the steps up to the churchyard, and the obvious ruins in the early nineteenth century drawings.

The mid-seventeenth century was thus a testing time for the village: the loss

5.3. Drawing of ruins which join the churchyard, probably of Cuddesdon Manor by C. Nattes (Bod. MS Top. Oxon. b.3 fol. 35)

of its two largest houses, which were presumably major sources of employment, contributed to a decline in Cuddesdon's population and influence. These were also years of disease: large numbers of premature deaths are recorded in the registers. In most years there were between 15 and 25 burials in the village, but in 1643 this increased to 73. The following year the figure remained high (68) reaching a peak with 28 burials taking place in September 1644: presumably a contagious disease had hit the village.[36] It is known that Asian influenza ('Camp Fever') was ravaging the soldiers around Oxford in this period.[37]

On 13 June 1646 the vicarage was sequestrated and Bishop Skinner was replaced by W. Beecher, who, not surprisingly, refused to acknowledge the appropriation of the vicarage to the see. Bishop Skinner was later cited for depredations on the vicarage and for retaining the tithes. It was also alleged that Skinner's son had molested Beecher.[38] A few years later at the time of the parliamentary survey in 1650/51 the incumbent was Robert Easton who was receiving £100 per annum from the tithes of hay and all the small tithe. The bishop's lands had been leased to William Child in 1650 who was paying a rent of £17 13s 6d.

At the Restoration of King Charles II in 1660, an act was passed indemnifying the destruction of property during the Civil Wars, which meant that the diocese was left without any redress for the destruction of the Palace. At the same time, however, letters patent returned the vicarage to the bishop in perpetuity. Also in 1660 Richard Skinner was restored as Bishop of Oxford and regained the rectorial income. He continued to reside at Launton until his translation to Worcester in 1662. Despite the Restoration, the future of Cuddesdon as a home for the Bishops of Oxford was far from secure.

NOTES

1   On Bancroft, who was educated at Westminster School and Christ Church, see Browne Willis, *Survey*, iii, p. 433; see also Marshall, *Oxford*, p. 122.

2   Hill, *Economic Conditions*, p. 316.

3   Wood, *Athenae Oxonienses*, ii, p. 894.

4   Cf Letters Patent, ORO ODP 1788. The vicarage was worth £17 4s 6d. This permission was later cited in the discussions when the vicarage was separated from the rectory in 1852. The Diocesan registry dates the permission as 27 February 1632.

5   *Calendar of State Papers (Domestic) 1636-7*, ed. John Bruce, London: Longmans, 1867, p. 507; *VCH*, v, p. 104.

6   *Calendar of State Papers (Domestic) 1636-7*, p. 507. The first fruits (annates) was the first year's income of the benefice. See also ORO CPR f. 65. Shotover at this stage was a royal forest.

7   *Calendar of State Papers (Domestic) 1636-7*, p. 507. ORO ODP c. 2148 f. 6.

8   In the original document the sum is now illegible, but seems to be either £2,300 or £2,500 (ORO ODP c. 2148 f. 6; see also *VCH*, v, p. 100; ii, p. 39). The state papers state £2,400. Browne Willis reckons £3,000, 'a great sum in regard to the Prices in building at this day' (*Survey*, iii, p. 433).

9   Browne Willis, *Survey*, iii, p. 418.

10   Wood, *Athenae Oxonienses*, ii, 894. The palace can be seen in the background of Bancroft's portrait. Rawlinson also made an etching of the palace around 1718.

11   Wood, *Athenae Oxonienses*, ii, p. 893.

12   *Calendar of State Papers (Domestic) 1636-7*, p. 114.

13   Browne Willis, *Survey*, iii, p. 433.

14   Browne Willis, *Survey*, iii, p. 418.

15   The Consecration deed for the Chapel, which is undated, is included with the diocesan papers: ORO ODP c. 2149 no. 1.

16   G. D. Squibb (ed.), *The Visitation of Oxfordshire 1669 and 1675 made by Sir Edward Bysshe, Kt*, London: Harleian Society, 1993, p. 36; cf. *VCH*, v, p. 107; cf. Wood, *Athenae Oxonienses*, iv, 839-42. An inventory of the house is included at Bod. MS Top Oxon c. 206.

17   *Calendar of State Papers (Domestic) 1636-7*, p. 507. ORO Oxf. Archd. Pp. Oxon c. 142 ff 31-33b.

18   Royal Instructions to the Episcopate first issued in 1629 and added to on 19 January 1635, reprinted in Kenneth Fincham (ed.) *Visitation Articles and Injunctions of the Early Stuart Church* II, Woodbridge: Boydell and Brewer (Church of England Record Society 5), 1994, p. 39.

19   ORO ODP c 2148 no. 7. After 1634, bishops who held livings in *commendam* were

required to account annually to the archbishop that they had not been disposed of (Hill, *Economic Problems*, p. 317).

20   ORO CPR b. 5 f. 2. Bod Tanner 147 fol. 73.

21   *Calendar of State Papers (Domestic) 1636-7*, pp. 507-8.

22   Wood, *Athenae Oxonienses*, ii, p.894, Marshall, *Oxford*, p.122.

23   ORO CPR b. 5 f. 2; Bod. Tanner 147 fol. 73.

24   ORO Archd. Oxon e. 12.

25   Wood, *Athenae Oxonienses*, ii, p. 893. This is confirmed in the register which also contains a flyleaf noting that the burial was 'under the south wall of the chancel'. Cf. Browne Willis, *Survey*, iii, p. 433.

26   In his *Life and Times*, Wood mentions searching through the registers of Cuddesdon for 1640 and 1641 for the day and year when Bancroft was buried. *The Life and Times of Anthony Wood, antiquary of Oxford, 1632-1695*, Oxford: Oxford Historical Society, 1892, Vol. II, (December 1680), p. 506. He also drew a picture of the Mill in 1681 (p. 562).

27   See above Plate 4.2.

28   His daughter Bridget was buried on 2 October 1643.

29   On the Civil War in the Oxford area see David Eddershaw, *The Civil War in Oxfordshire*, Stroud: Alan Sutton, 1995.

30   'On the north side of ye. Church was lately ye. Bishops house of Oxon: demolisht in ye. Warr time: as alsoe Sr Tho. Gardiners home on ye. south side of ye church, he himself burning it for feare ye parliamenteirs should make a garrison of it against the king' (*Life and Times*, p.107). Browne Willis notes that the house 'did not long outlast the generous Founder' (Browne Willis, *Survey*, iii, p. 433).

31   *VCH*, v, p. 98. See John Fox, 'Wheatley Bridge and the English Civil War' in Fox, *One More Millennium*, pp. 18-20.

32   Wood, *Athenae Oxonienses*, ii, p. 894.

33   *VCH*, v, p. 100.

34   For the history of Cuddesdon Manor, see *VCH*, v, p. 102. In 1821 the Manor was in the hands of Sir James Whalley Smythe Gardiner, although it was a matter of some debate whether this Gardiner was a descendant of the Gardiners of the earlier period. See *Gentleman's Magazine* Vol. XCI (May, 1821), p. 395. A plaque to a Mrs Smythe was moved from the chancel in Pott's restoration.

35   *VCH*, v, p. 101.

36   A note is included in the 1644 burials register drawing attention to the large number of burials. (ORO CPR c. 2 f. 54).

37   Fox, *One More Millennium*, p. 18.

38   A. G. Matthews (ed.), *Walker Revised: Being a revision of John Walker's Sufferings of the Clergy During the Grand Rebellion, 1642-60*, Oxford: Clarendon, 1948, p. 12.

Chapter Six

From the Restoration to Wilberforce

The Rebuilding of the Palace

Cuddesdon's parlous ecclesiastical state was not to last long: Bishop Skinner's successor, William Paul, who had been a chaplain to Charles I, becoming Dean of Lichfield at the Restoration, made plans for the rebuilding of the palace at Cuddesdon. Archbishop Sheldon allowed him to retain his rectory at Brightwell in order to secure sufficient finance for the reconstruction of the palace – it seems that all that was left of the original palace was a large fireplace. He got as far as providing timber but died in 1665 before work could be carried out.[1] Paul was succeeded by Walter Blandford, who soon brought an action against Rachael Paul, his predecessor's widow, claiming that the £1,997 which was required for repairs to the palace should be taken from the revenues which had been collected during her husband's episcopate. She submitted a detailed defence, challenging Blandford's estimate and claiming both that repairs could be carried out for £1,500 and also (and accurately) that the destruction had been wrought before her husband's time. A very precise estimate for the building work survives. Rachael Paul also claimed that the episcopal revenues were insufficient to raise enough money for the palace after the payment of the first fruits and the expenses of the curate in Cuddesdon. She also noted that her husband had amassed between £200 and £300 worth of timber which Blandford had not taken into account. Bishop Paul's predecessor, Robert Skinner, came to her assistance, noting the act of indemnity of 1660.[2] In the end it would seem that Blandford lost his case, since nothing more was done to the palace until the time of John Fell who became Bishop of Oxford in 1676.

Fell had been Dean of Christ Church and was a noted scholar who edited an important early edition of the Greek New Testament. He was also regarded as a man who, despite his many gifts, failed to gain popularity among those he served. Nevertheless, as with many present-day Oxford heads

6.1. Cuddesdon Palace in 1820 before Wilberforce's Extensions by J. Buckler (Bod. MS Top. Oxon. a. 66 fol. 207)

of houses, he had gifts as a money raiser and administrator and in 1679 set about the reconstruction of the palace with 'moneys out of his own purse ... upon the old foundation with a chapel in it as before',[3] 'yet he enjoyed but a little time in it'.[4] He made use of Bishop Paul's timber, employing a number of craftsmen whose services he had previously used in Christ Church. These included Richard Frogley, the College's master carpenter who was employed at Cuddesdon 'by the Great', that is as a chief contractor who then sub-contracted to the various tradesmen. Thomas Wood, a stonemason, was also employed, although he seems to have been preoccupied in building the Old Ashmolean Museum (now the Museum of the History of Science) in Broad Street. There was a lengthy dispute between Frogley and Wood[5] which led to the contract for the new chapel going to a local man, Thomas Chapman. This chapel stood on the same site as Bancroft's original, some of which still appears to have been standing.[6] Fell was able to see the outside of the palace completed and limewashed by the end of 1679.[7]

A plan of the old palace was drawn up during Wilberforce's extensions by his architect, Benjamin Ferrey.[8] Taking into account Bishop Secker's improvements in the eighteenth century, Bishop Fell's palace was a large plain H-shaped symmetrical stone house of two storeys with a third storey of gabled windows. The court dispute between the contractors reveals that Burford stone was used in its construction. The main entrance was on the north side, the great hall in the centre, and library and chapel in the north part of the east wing. A little parlour, which was later a chaplain's room, was situated in the south-east corner of the house, and there was another larger parlour to the south-west. There was a passage under the stairs which led down to the old cellars, which also provided the menservants' quarters.[9]

The interior of the house is not as well documented, although the chapel had black and white marble flooring, and the hall is recorded as having a chequered pavement. Jennifer Sherwood sums up the building as 'owing much to Dutch Palladianism, common in England c.1700 but an advanced design at this date'.[10] *The Gentleman's Magazine* of 1821 described the palace as 'of no great architectural pretensions, but possessing an agreeable situation and prospect'.[11] There were also (probably) two fine gate posts which were later incorporated into the imposing doorway to the north side of the house of Wilberforce's rebuilding. This was taken down after the 1958 fire and re-assembled at Christ Church, Oxford as the entrance to Blue Boar quadrangle from the south end of the south range of Peckwater Quad.[12] Apart from the Victorian chapel and remains of a stable block (both of which have been considerably altered in recent years), this is all that now remains of the palace.

After his death in 1686, Fell was succeeded by Bishop Samuel Parker, who played a leading part in James II's attempts to reform the religion of England to Roman Catholicism.[13] He was considered by Richard Congreve, chaplain to Bishop John Hough (Parker's far from sympathetic successor), as a

> man of learning and parts but was thought to have little religion. It was claimed that his eldest son had a little horse that ran in the churchyard at Cuddesdon, which, as he endeavoured several times to drive out into the church porch, the horse still turned away from it and would not go in. "On my conscience" says the boy, "It seemeth to me that the horse liketh the church as little as my Right Reverend Father".[14]

After this time, the Palace was lived in by the Bishops of Oxford through the eighteenth and nineteenth centuries (although some were more frequent residents in Cuddesdon than others). Consequently from the time of Bishop Fell Cuddesdon's history was once again intricately bound up with the bishops of Oxford.

Cuddesdon and the Church in the Eighteenth Century

The eighteenth century has often been regarded as a period when the Church of England was at a low ebb: non-residency (where the clergyman did not reside in his parish) and pluralism (where he held more than one ecclesi-

6.2. Gates to Bishop's Palace (anonymous) (RCC)

astical office) were common, and many clergymen supposedly lacked diligence in performing their duties. However, perhaps because of Cuddesdon's unusual status with the bishop having appropriated the vicarage and living in the village, it would appear that the church building was relatively well-maintained and that services were frequent. There were, however, periods when the Cuddesdon church records were lost, when presumably the clergy were less conscientious. Thomas Fulkes, for instance, seems to have lost or destroyed the baptismal register for 1668 since William Hunt's baptismal record was lost, as a sworn statement of 16 Oct 1695 notes. There are virtually no entries in the registers from 1645 to 1681, and again from 1701-1721. After this date record keeping improved significantly: numbers of baptisms hovered around twenty annually, declining slightly to around twelve in the early nineteenth century. Burials were fairly constant at around fifteen annually through the eighteenth century, with an occasional higher number as in 1750 when there were thirty-five deaths.[15]

Even during the times when records were lost, however, the building was used significantly more frequently than many other parish churches in the diocese at the time: in 1705, for instance, there were no fewer than 8 celebrations of holy communion, a very large number for those days. Indeed this pattern seems to have been the norm right through the eighteenth century. In a detailed visitation return of 1778, the curate, John Parkman, noted that communion was celebrated at Christmas, Palm Sunday, Easter Day, Low Sunday, Whitsunday, and twice at Michaelmas. The number receiving communion on Sundays was between 20 and 40. In addition to two regular Sunday services, when a sermon was preached in the morning, prayers were also said on Wednesdays and Fridays, 'except a saint's day fall on some other day, in which case it has been usual to read prayers on that day instead'. The curate also personally catechised the children every Sunday in Lent. By way of comparison, Thomas Secker, Bishop of Oxford from 1737 to 1758 laid down rules for the diocese in 1741 which included a minimum of four celebrations of communion per year, as well as a requirement to hold divine service on Wednesdays, Fridays and holy days. Presumably many churches were failing to comply with even these modest requirements. Cuddesdon, on the other hand, was more than fulfilling its duties.

Given that there does not seem to have been a stipend reserved for the curate—the appropriate section of the visitation returns is often left blank—it is likely that the church was served by a curate whose primary duty was as chaplain or secretary to the bishop; by the mid-eighteenth century Wheatley was usually (although not always) treated separately in visitations, although occasionally the curate of Wheatley (as in 1784) is also included in the

Cuddesdon returns. Several patterns emerge from the visitations: there were frequent changes to the Cuddesdon clergy, although most seem to have been resident, presumably working for the bishop. This was again a relatively unusual phenomenon in the Oxford area where nearby villages were frequently served by fellows of Colleges. In the time of Richard Rawlinson (1690-1755), Daniel Slaymaker, a graduate of Magdalen College, Oxford[16] was officiating in the church, and it was noted that an 'allowance to the minister is a voluntary contribution'.[17] A brief note in the Banns book, however, indicates non-residence in 1772. On 7 January, it was noted, Herbert Randolph could not call banns: 'There being no duty at Cuddesdon on that day by reason of a great fall of snow which rendered the road between Cuddesdon and Oxford impassable.'

In the 1802 visitation the curate claimed a stipend of £60 per annum, although others, including Richard Budd in 1805, and H. Bishop in 1823, seem to have survived solely on fees for burials. Few mention a house, although J. Ballard, curate in 1808 occupied a house with a garden. He also had a stipend of £60. The church continued to be used far more than most other churches of the time, often serving as a centre for confirmations for the Cuddesdon deanery, and possibly for an even wider area. This might explain the 18s that was spent on two gallons of wine in 1771 as well as the new paten which was donated in the same year by L. Lucas, the curate.[18] On 2 August 1778 no fewer than 300 people were confirmed in the church during the epis-copacy of the Tory pamphleteer John Butler, and a similar number were confirmed in 1781. 100 more were confirmed on 31 August 1788, and a further 200 two years later. A similar number was maintained for most years well into the nineteenth century. The largest number was in 1796 when 360 were confirmed during the episcopate of Edward Smallwell.

The churchwardens' accounts exist from 1705. These, together with the visitation returns, reveal something about the life of the parish. The main expenditure was on the fabric, closely followed by the bells with the costs of communions, services and vestments next, but a long way behind.[19] In 1755, for instance, 9s 3d. was spent on wine at Easter and 19s. 6d. on new bell ropes. The bells were always a major item of expenditure, both for repairs and for peels: in 1722 the cost of the peel rung at the coronation of George I was 3s. 4d. and in 1769 £12 7s 0d. was paid to Mr Turner, the bell hanger. Other expenditure was on rather less obviously ecclesiastical items including catching hedgehogs (at the rate of 4d. each) and foxes at the somewhat higher rate of 1s: the parish still retained important secular functions. Later in the century a large amount of work had to be done to the roof and to the windows, and in 1770 116 feet of oak was purchased. A clock built by John

Smith and Sons of Derby was added in 1776. This was followed by a weather cock in 1789 at the cost of £1 18s,[20] when the clock dial was also regilded. Receipts for the first years of the eighteenth century averaged about £8. This came almost wholly from the church rate from Cuddesdon, Denton and Wheatley, the latter two townships contributing identical amounts.[21]

Some visitations (as for instance in 1733) simply reported that all was well with the church, whereas others are more detailed.[22] The fabric of the Church seems to have deteriorated late in the eighteenth century, so much so that by 1788 Archdeacon George Turner did not make the usual declaration 'all is well'. Instead he wrote an additional note after the visitation returns for 23 October 1790: the then churchwardens, William Webb and Richard Rogers were 'admonished to repair the church doors and the pillars of the gallery, and to paint the gallery by the first day of January instant and to certify having made the repairs by the fifteenth of the said month'.[23] As the churchwardens did not appear in person at the visitation, none apparently having been chosen, a Joseph Calloway was appointed, who in 1791 asked for the period of time to be extended 'to the first day of next Easter term'. It would seem that the repairs cost £5 6s. 10*d.* which was paid to a carpenter in 1791, and £1 0s 2*d.* to the blacksmith. By 1801, things had evidently improved and the church walls had been repaired. Other repairs and improvements were made in the next few years: in 1828, for instance, a large sum was paid out for building the new vestry in the small room created next to the tower stairs,[24] and in 1831 £81 3s 10½*d.* was paid to a carpenter for the restoration of the west gallery, but which lasted only a few years before it was removed. Church finances also seem to have increased with the total Church rate rising to £37 19s. 8¾*d.* In 1835, during Denison's time as curate, it was again reported that 'All belonging to this parish is in good repair'.

Thomas Secker, bishop from 1737-58, made improvements to the Palace, including increasing the size of the living accommodation, and laying out a pleasure garden to the south-east. He was also responsible for moving the chapel to the south-west corner of the house. It is also likely that the fine stucco fireplace which survived until the fire of 1958 may well have been made at this time by the Oxford plasterer, Thomas Roberts, who produced the plasterwork in the Upper Library at Christ Church. A new drawing room and dining room were also probably added during Secker's time, together with a courtyard on the west side of the house.[25] Secker, who went on to become Archbishop of Canterbury, is described tactfully by Marshall as 'a man of high respectability rather than of eminent talent' who, as is clear from the improvements he made to his palace, was evidently concerned with his material as much as his spiritual well-being.[26]

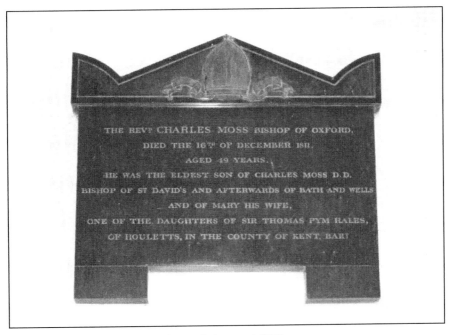

THE REVᴰ CHARLES MOSS BISHOP OF OXFORD,
DIED THE 16ᵀᴴ OF DECEMBER 1811.
AGED 49 YEARS.
HE WAS THE ELDEST SON OF CHARLES MOSS D.D.
BISHOP OF Sᵗ DAVID'S AND AFTERWARDS OF BATH AND WELLS
AND OF MARY HIS WIFE,
ONE OF THE DAUGHTERS OF SIR THOMAS PYM HALES,
OF HOULETTS, IN THE COUNTY OF KENT, BARᵗ

6.3. Bishop Moss's monument in south transept (MC)

Although Cuddesdon remained a village profoundly influenced by the Bishops of Oxford, it did not escape the attention of John Wesley. On 30 November 1789 he visited Cuddesdon, where, while visiting a poor family for breakfast, he was reminded of his own upbringing in a large family. He wrote movingly in his diary:

> In my way to Wycombe I spent an hour at Mr Smith's[27] in Cuddesdon. He has ten children, from eighteen to a year or two old, but all under government; so that I met the very picture of my father's family. What a picture of my father's family. What a wretched steward was he who influenced Lord Harcourt to put away such a tenant.[28]

Cuddesdon in the Early Nineteenth Century

In the nineteenth century Cuddesdon continued to play a prominent role in the lives of the Bishops of Oxford. Charles Moss, an immensely wealthy man, who was bishop from 1807-11 and was buried in the church,[29] contributed no less than £3,000 for the maintenance of schools at Wheatley and Cuddesdon. These were supported by the recently formed National Society. A permanent school at Cuddesdon was not built until 1841, but one at Wheatley was opened in 1819 and for a time served some of the children

6.4. Legge's hatchment (now in ringing chamber) (MC)

of Cuddesdon. Prior to this date education at Cuddesdon had been catered for by a charity school, which in 1790 had 18 children.[30] In 1793 there was a Sunday School, described as 'recently set up'.[31] By 1802 there was 'a private school at the Lord Bishop of Oxford's discretion'[32] which may perhaps be the same as the Charity School for 'twelve poor girls' noted in Cox's *History*.[33] In 1818 there were two private schools with forty pupils each, although it was noted in a House of Commons report that there was inadequate provision for poor children.[34] One of the private schools survived in Cuddesdon in 1833 with 16 boys and 40 girls paying 3*d*. each, half of which was contributed by the bishop. It is feasible that some of the poorer children attended school in Wheatley, since it was noted later in the century that the vicar of Wheatley complained that the more respectable children tended to go to school in Cuddesdon.[35] The village of Cuddesdon itself, however, was far from wealthy: as late as 1832 four deaths are recorded from cholera.

In the detailed reply to the Bishop's 1805 Visitation questions,[36] Richard Budd, the Cuddesdon curate noted that there were no dissenters and only one 'papist', and also that there were no 'intentional absences' from Church. Nevertheless he also noted (somewhat pompously) that 'Too many absent themselves through indolence or an attention to worldly concerns'. In 1823, however, there seems to have been some non-conformist activity in

Cuddesdon. Although there were still no 'papists' noted in the visitation return, the curate, H. Bishop, noted: 'Very recently a few persons have had a house licensed for public worship which is attended by itinerant preachers ... There are, however, but few who attend this "cottage".' Although there is no indication where this meeting house might have been, it is likely that it was located somewhere in Cuddesdon, since Wheatley was treated separately at this point and had its own chapel. Perhaps more important is the large rise in numbers of Church of England communicants which increased from 217 in 1820 to 294 in 1822. Numbers of communions had also increased to ten by 1829. Cuddesdon Church was undoubtedly thriving in the first part of the nineteenth century.

The only surviving funerary hatchment in Cuddesdon dates from 1827 and commemorates Bishop Edward Legge. It is an unusual example in that it displays the arms of the bishop as well as those of the diocese and All Souls' College, where he remained warden. Hatchments were displayed on the outside of the deceased's residence during the period of mourning; they were then often placed in the parish church. Another hatchment exists for Legge at All Souls' College in Oxford.[37] Legge's successor was Charles Lloyd (bishop from 1827-1829 and also Regius Professor of Divinity) who used to hold informal meetings at Cuddesdon for his clergy and their wives. William Ewart Gladstone, who was at Christ Church during this time and regularly visited Cuddesdon, commented that Lloyd was 'a man of powerful talents, and of a character both winning and decided, who, had his life been spared, might have acted powerfully for good on the fortunes of the Church of England, by guiding the energetic influence which his teaching had done so much to form.'[38] Lloyd was extremely influential on Pusey, Newman and other members of the Oxford Movement.

Lloyd's successor in 1829 was Richard Bagot, sixth son of Lord Bagot, whom Newman described as a 'man of noble mind, and as kind-hearted as he was noble'. He continued to reside for much of the time in the family living of Blithfield in Staffordshire, finding Cuddesdon inaccessible and inconvenient. 'There is but one road to the place,' he wrote in defence of his attempt to move the see house to Shotover, 'and this at times during the winter nearly impassable, with the exception of the cart-road through the fields, which may be used in summer-time, but then with great difficulty'.[39] Once again the finances of the see were in a poor state and in order to supplement his income he had to retain prebends of Lichfield, Worcester and Windsor along with the deanery of Canterbury. He was forced into this position primarily because of the abuses associated with the granting of leases (often as long as a lifetime) for so-called 'fines'. A large portion of the revenues of the see could thereby be anticipated by the bishop who had originally granted the lease, without provision made for successors in the see: this meant the annual revenues of the see were accordingly reduced. Although such abuses were abolished by the ecclesiastical reforms later in the 1830s, their effect was to stifle the missionary work of the Church of England during this time of rapid social change. Oxford's episcopal revenues were finally put in order only in 1850. In a letter of 1845, Bagot's successor, Samuel Wilberforce noted that the Ecclesiastical 'Commissioners pay to this diocese, not taking anything from it, because it is so poor. They are to make it up to £5,000 a year. But for the next 5 years, I shall be very poor.'[40]

Despite the financial problems of the see, however, Bishop Bagot was a conscientious and respected bishop, who made careful provision for the exercise of ministry in the village of Cuddesdon: during his time there were some notable curates. Augustus Page Saunders (1801-78) went on to become headmaster of Charterhouse in 1832, and later Dean of Peterborough. Saunders' successor was George Denison (1805-96) who retained a fellowship at Oriel College but who also kept two cottages in the village tutoring students during the vacations, and then moving more or less permanently to the village from 1836 until 1838 when he left to become incumbent at Broadwindsor in Dorset. At the time a Sunday School was held in the church since there was no schoolroom in the village. It is also interesting to note that Henry Manning, later Archdeacon of Chichester (and after his conversion to Rome, Cardinal Archbishop of Westminster), preached his first sermon on Christmas Day 1832 shortly after his ordination as a deacon in Cuddesdon church.

Denison seems to have been prone to mishaps. In 1836 his mother gave him a medicine chest for use among the poor. His prowess as a doctor, however, was not great. Samuel Wilberforce later used to insist at dinner parties that the erstwhile hapless curate (by then the eminent Archdeacon of Taunton) relate the story of the time he gave a large dose of laudanum to a ninety-year old woman which made her sit up in bed and sing. Denison also put a stove into the crossing of the church. A flue ran to the north-east corner of the north transept, passing through the wall over the wall plate. On a Christmas day the stove was burning as Denison went to read the first lesson. There was some commotion and Denison asked what it was about. The clerk responded: 'Please, sir. If you don't stop reading we shall all be burnt alive ... the church be on fire'. Unperturbed Denison announced: 'there is a little accident, you had better go out and get ladders and plenty of water'. At that point the roof burst into flames, but was successfully extinguished.[41] Denison went on to become one of the most prominent high churchmen of the Victorian period, and was unsuccessfully prosecuted for maintaining the doctrine of the real presence in the eucharist in a famous case of 1854-8.

After Denison's departure the Church was served from 1839 by Bishop Bagot's chaplain, A. Goldney, who obtained the site from the Earl of Macclesfield for the National (i.e. Church) School in 1841, which was opened in 1847.[42] By the time of the 1854 visitation there were 67 boys and girls in the mixed juniors and 36 infants being taught in the school.[43] By 1906 rolls had fallen to only 59 pupils. Despite pleading from the Bishop-elect, Samuel Wilberforce, Goldney left to go with Bagot to Bath and Wells in 1845 as vicar of East Pennard, Somerset.[44] It was in the energetic episcopate of Bagot's successor, Wilberforce that Cuddesdon entered a new phase of its history.

NOTES

1   Wood, *Athenae Oxonienses*, ii, p. 895; cf. iv, p. 827. Paul died at Chinnor on 24 May 1665, and was moved to Brightwell for burial (Browne Willis, *Survey*, iii, p. 433).

2   On this see J. C. Cole, 'The Building of the Second Palace at Cuddesdon' in *Oxoniensia* 24-5 (1959-60), pp. 49-69, p. 50. Cf. Thomas Cox, *A Topographical, Ecclesiastical and Natural History of Oxfordshire*, Savoy, 1700, p. 408.

3   Wood, *Athenae Oxonienses*, ii, p. 894, 5.

4   Wood, *Athenae Oxonienses*, iv, p. 197. Fell initiated other building projects, including St Oswald's Hospital, Worcester. He also introduced reforms into Oxford worship, instituting daily prayers at St Martin's Church, Carfax (Browne Willis, *Survey*, iii, p. 435).

5   For full details of the dispute, which seems to have been common in building work at the time, see Cole, 'The Building of the Second Palace', pp. 63-9.

6   Watercolours of the Palace Bod MS Top. Oxon. b.220, f.70. The same page also contains an engraving of the first palace; another poor watercolour of the palace is at Bod. MS Top. Oxon. a.42, f.14.

7   Cole, 'The Building of the Second Palace,' p. 57; Wood, *Athenae Oxonienses*, ii. p. 895.

8   ORO ODP c. 2114 (1). See Cole, 'The Building of the Second Palace,' p. 59.

9   Cole, 'The Building of the Second Palace,' pp. 60-1.

10   Sherwood and Pevsner, *Oxfordshire*, p. 128.

11   *Gentleman's Magazine* XCI (Jan, 1821), p. 9.

12   Sherwood and Pevsner, *Oxfordshire*, p. 128.

13   Wood, *Athenae Oxonienses*, iv, pp. 225-35.

14   Table Talk of Bishop Hough as recorded by his chaplain, Richard Congreve, cited in Wood, *Athenae Oxonienses*, iv, p. 898.

15   A copy of the statistics sent to the Cambridge Centre for the History of Population and Social Structure, compiled in 1965, is contained in the Parish Archives.

16   John R. Bloxham (ed.), *The Register of St Mary Magdalen's College*, Oxford, Oxford: Graham, 1853, i. 124. Slaymaker or Sleamaker was also curate of Horspath in 1717.

17   F. N. Davis (ed.), *Parochial Collections made by Anthony à Wood, MA and Richard Rawlinson*, ORS 2, 1920, p. 106.

18   ORO Terrier 1913. This disappeared after being kept safe at the college, reappearing in a strong box on two occasions, in 1971 (PCC *Minute Book* 1970-87, p. 25) and

2002. A small alms dish of 1813 was rediscovered at the same time, as was a silver flagon of 1920. The valuation in 1971 was £380.

19   It was normal at the time for the churchwardens to supply the surplice for the officiating clergyman.

20   A replica was set up in 1953 to commemorate the coronation of Queen Elizabeth II.

21   In 1710, for instance, the rate was £3 17s. 4d. for Cuddesdon, and £2 2s. 6d. each for Wheatley and Denton. The rates fluctuated greatly throughout the century, ranging from over £11 for Cuddesdon in 1750 to just over £5 in 1783.

22   No entry was made for Cuddesdon in the 1738 visitation of Thomas Secker, nor in that of 1759. The only mention of Cuddesdon parish in Bishop Fell's book of 1708 is of several homes belonging to the poor at Wheatley. Fell presumably knew Cuddesdon too intimately to have to record details.

23   ORO Archd. Oxon. e. 12 p. 183.

24   See Parker's Plan, above Plate 3.8.

25   Cole, 'The Building of the Second Palace', p. 60.

26   Marshall, *Oxford*, p. 172.

27   The only Smith noted in the register was Thomas Smith (d. 1799) who was married to Ann (d. 1800). Their two year old, James was baptised on 31 May 1787.

28   Nehemiah Curnock (ed.), *The Journal of the Rev. John Wesley AM*, London: Epworth, 1938, viii, p. 21. The man had presumably been displaced from his home during Harcourt's remodelling of the village of Nuneham Courtenay.

29   The registers note that he was buried 'within the rail of the communion table close to the north wall of the chancel; the south side of the brick grave made for him is close to the north wall of the vault belonging to the family of the Gardiners'.

30   ORO ODP Bishop's Visitation 1790.

31   ORO ODP b. 9. Bishop's Visitation 1793.

32   ORO ODP d. 566. Bishop's Visitation, 1802.

33   Thomas Cox, *A Topographical, Ecclesiastical and Natural History of Oxfordshire*, p. 498.

34   *VCH*, v, p. 99.

35   *VCH*, v, p. 99.

36   ORO ODP, d. 568 f. 107.

37   Peter Summers (ed.), *Hatchments of Britain*, London: Phillimore, 1974-94, iv, p. 834.

38   *A Chapter of Autobiography*, London: John Murray, 1868, p. 53.

39   G. F. A. Best, *Temporal Pillars*, Cambridge: Cambridge University Press, 1964, p. 364.

40   Letter to Louisa Noel, 9 Nov 1845 cited in A. R. Ashwell, *Life of Bishop Wilberforce*, London: John Murray, 1880, i, p. 310.

41   George Anthony Denison, *Notes of My Life*, 1805-1878, London: James Parker, 1878, p. 75 cited in Joyce Coombs, *George Anthony Denison. The Firebrand*, London: Faith Press, 1984, pp. 17-18.

42   ORO ODP c. 447 f. 91.

43   *VCH* (v, p. 99) reports that 'about 30 infants' were being taught in a cottage in Church Road by Rebecca Allen, although there is no indication of this on the visitation return.

44   Letter to Goldney, 17 Nov 1845 in R. K. Pugh (ed.), *The Letter-Books of Samuel Wilberforce* ORS 47, 1970, pp. 47-8.

Chapter Seven

Samuel Wilberforce and the Heyday of Cuddesdon

Samuel Wilberforce and Cuddesdon

In 1846 Samuel Wilberforce succeeded to the diocese of Oxford, which had been much enlarged to include both Berkshire and Buckinghamshire. In Wilberforce, Oxford gained a man of extraordinary vigour, with an enormous gift for organisation, who transformed virtually everything he touched. In his last charge to the diocese before his translation to Winchester in 1869 he noted that 250 churches had been erected or restored and that over £2,000,000 had been spent on building. This compares with fewer than twenty new churches in the 600 years between 1220 and 1820.[1] Cuddesdon was certainly not exempt from his reforming zeal.

As bishop-elect he went to stay with Bishop Bagot and Lady Harriet from 7 to 10 November 1845 to inspect his new house. He wrote to Louisa Noel in his typically pithy style:

I was very courteously received by the Bishop and Lady Harriet (Lady Jersey's sister). The palace is not a bit of a palace. It is an old H-shaped house, a rambling sort of country gentleman's house, very small grounds, but a pretty garden, very unmagnificent. There is a nice lawn, with fine old elms, and a very pretty church close by. I *am* Rector, and like very much keeping up with that pastoral character our Bishops are so apt to lose. There is a curate, who of course must be the effective parish priest during a great part of the year. But it will be my flock. It is 500 *quite* agricultural people. This, I greatly like, and think it will be very useful for my dear children. It is, so far, more true country than Alvestoke. The house stands almost on the top of a high hill of sand, very dry and healthy, sheltered from the N.E., except for the elms round it (150 years old, and noble fellows), and the church, to E., S., and W., with a fine panoramic view, looking over the chalk hills of Buckinghamshire, Oxfordshire (Checkendon), and Berks. Behind it is

7.1. Samuel Wilberforce as Bishop of Oxford (RCC)

Shotover, rising very gently a *little* higher to the north; one of the noblest *terraces* for walking and riding in all England. The gardens & c., seem small, and productive, and 2 men do them; a little land, but no Manors or anything great – all of which I think quite good for me and less expensive I hope than if otherwise. I had a walk alone, after church this morning, on Shotover, and many deep, and awful, and hopeful thoughts. May God bring them to a good issue.[2]

Shortly after his consecration Wilberforce began reconstructing the palace on a more generous scale, successfully pressing both the Archbishop of Canterbury and the Ecclesiastical Commissioners for funds. By this stage Bishop Bagot seems to have changed his mind about Cuddesdon as a suitable residence for the bishop and assisted Wilberforce in his appeal for funds.[3] On the initial meeting about the improvements, the Commissioners were shown the plans made by Wilberforce's architect, Benjamin Ferrey, but they suggested to the bishop that he might consider Shotover House as a more suitable residence. However, what Best called the 'last gasp of independence' on the part of the Commissioners was unsuccessful and on 28 January 1846 £3,500 was approved for expenditure on the palace, and a further £1,300 for the demesne (estate). As usual, however, the estimates proved rather modest, and Wilberforce reported on 18 March 1847 that the improvements had cost £1,836 in excess. An application was made for a mortgage, which was granted, which meant that the architect was eventually paid.[4]

Part of the expenditure was on a 'new and very neat' detached chapel 'in the early-English style of architecture … for the convenience of the Bishop's household'.[5] This was consecrated by Wilberforce assisted by Bishop Field of Newfoundland, and Dr Phillimore on 10 December 1846 and dedicated to SS. Peter and Paul. Several leading members of the University were present, as was a large body of neighbouring parochial clergy.[6] The bishop himself preached the sermon which is highly informative about his vision for Cuddesdon as a place of spiritual refreshment and renewal:

For as the bishop's dwelling-place is not his private house, but the common property of all his diocese, held only in trust by him for them, to be the common centre, at which from every part the scattered pastors may meet together with him for counsel, thought, deliberation, and united action: so is the chapel at this place theirs as well as his: theirs at their special meeting here, that they may withdraw from the world, here together watch, pray, and communicate, and hence return strengthened and refreshed to meet their common toils and ordinary dangers: theirs at the ordination seasons, that here before their vows are sealed openly

Above 7.2. Bishop's Palace from the driveway after Wilberforce's alterations (COS)
Below 7.3. Palace from the garden side showing new chapel (RCC)

in the cathedral church, the candidates for ordination may day by day be brought, in the reading of God's word, by prayer, and communion, beneath the healing and refreshing dews of God's most Holy Spirit. And theirs also for another reason, that as they have all an interest in their bishop's spiritual welfare, that as they will be blessed by wise counsels, a holy example, earnest intercessions, grave rebukes, tender encouragements; and as they will be blighted if dimness of sight in matters spiritual, coldness, coarseness, secularity, worldliness, or sloth be here enthroned; it is their special interest as well as his, that within these walls God may indeed be continually sought and always found. For how can any one but faintly hope to bear this change, unless he be a man of fervent and continual prayer?[7]

The Chapel building so eulogised, which is the only part of the palace still standing, (although with a much changed interior from its days as part of a retreat house run by Toc H, and more recently as a private house), is a simple rectangular structure.[8] It was built by Benjamin Ferrey in the decorated style with a small bell turret at the east end and two west windows containing heraldic shields of the Bishop and the Prince Consort by Thomas Willement, one of the pioneers of the revival of the medieval tradition of glass design. The glass was the gift of Queen Victoria and Prince Albert, and the Archbishops of Canterbury and York.[9] The bishop used the chapel regularly for private meditations. On 14 July 1863, for instance, he recalled his life, vowing (rather morbidly) to 'strive to live more in the sight of Death' and 'to commend myself more entirely as dying creature into the hand of the only Lord of Life'.[10]

In an act which reflected something of the ambitious vision expressed in the consecration sermon, Wilberforce built a sizeable extension to the palace to allow him to house all his ordinands during the annual pre-ordination retreat. This extension masked something of the picturesque form of the house. Throughout his ministry Wilberforce took a particular interest in ordination candidates: he was keen on having them 'as much as possible under my own eye, and to secure all opportunities of social, friendly and spiritual intercourse'.[11] Candidates were to assemble for three days at Cuddesdon and were then to be examined. On a visit to Cuddesdon in 1851, Christopher Wordsworth remarked that no fewer than fifty candidates for ordination were gathered together in the palace. Wilberforce's goal in these improvements was to be able to bring his ordinands and clergy together so that they could hear what he had to tell them and how best they might assist him. At the same time there was a large number of eminent visitors to the palace, Wilberforce's diary recording a constant round of social engagements. There was no little controversy over the enlargement of an already sizeable palace. An Oxfordshire incumbent, Thomas Fosbery, complaining of the expense on the Palace, received a reply from Wilberforce that extra space was needed to accommodate candidates for orders, and, besides, he had done nothing excessive or indulged in unnecessary luxury. There was, he claimed, 'nothing of finery or decoration'.[12] Wilberforce's vision was both strong and authoritative.

7.4. Bishop's Chapel in 2003 (MC)

Alfred Pott and the Restoration of the Church

Not long after the rebuilding of the palace, Wilberforce set about re-organ-
ising pastoral care in the village. Initially he employed William Thomson as
curate whom he had offered the curacy of Alverstoke shortly before his
appointment to Oxford. Thomson stayed only a few months before moving
to Oxford as Chaplain of Queen's College, and going on to become successively Bishop of Gloucester and Archbishop of York.[13] After Thomson's
departure he chose Alfred Pott (1822-1908) to be curate of the village in 1847.
Pott, who went on to become vicar of Abingdon and then Archdeacon of
Berkshire, was educated at Eton and Magdalen College, Oxford and elected
President of the Oxford Union in 1845. Initially he lived at the house known
as the Old Vicarage,[14] although at the time there was no 'vicar' of the parish.

Almost immediately the young clergyman, who had only been ordained in
December 1845, began to appeal for subscribers for a restoration of the church
influenced by the latest 'ecclesiological' style. He aimed to transform the
church into a model church for the diocese, continuing the modest work
begun by his predecessor in 1842 which was mentioned by Parker in his 1846

guide which notes that a pulpit and lectern had been removed. It is also likely that the screen immediately before the crossing, which probably dates from the early the seventeenth century, was removed in this first period of restoration. The screen can be clearly seen in the drawing made by G. Hollis for the *Gentleman's Magazine* in 1821, but does not appear in Parker's drawings.[15] The *Victoria County History* mistakenly attributes this first period of restoration to G. E. Street, who had yet to establish himself as an architect.[16]

The first discussions about a full restoration date from 1843, when an application was made by Bishop Bagot to the Oxford Historical and Architectural Society to seek their advice. The Society, which resembled the Cambridge Camden Society of Benjamin Webb and J. M. Neale, had been established principally to advance the study of Gothic architecture and had become an unofficial (and highly opinionated) advisory board for church restoration projects. The General Committee of the Society, it was reported, 'will authorize the architect of the Society to go to Cuddesdon and recommend a new East window for the Chancel, also to examine the church generally and recommend restorations which may be gradually effected'. The Committee was also charged with an examination of Dorchester Abbey, a project which took up much time and energy in the next few years.[17]

It is not clear whether this initial visit resulted in immediate action, but any

7.5. The Old Vicarage in about 1900 (COS)

7.6. Alfred Pott. First Vicar of Cuddesdon and Principal of Cuddesdon College (RCC)

restoration must have been modest, since on 15 Nov 1848 Pott published a handbill commenting on the state in which he had found the building and summarising his ambitious plans:

> The peculiar character and beauty of many of its details, have long rendered it a subject of great regret, that it should remain in the unworthy condition to which the bad taste of by-gone days has reduced it, and from which it has hardly at all emerged. To those who know the Church it will be needless to state in detail the many disfigurements under which it labours. The fine central tower has been crowned with a modern parapet and sham pinnacles; in the interior, the whole West end is choked up with a useless and most offensive gallery; the body of the

church is in several parts disfigured with high pews; the Reading Desk and Pulpit are so placed as to render the voice inaudible in the Chancel and Transepts. The groining under the Central Tower has been destroyed and superseded by a timber ringing gallery; the open roofs of the transepts have been concealed by lath and plaster ceilings. Above all, the Chancel is in such a state as to require remodelling and refitting through its whole extent. It is proposed to enter to the work without delay.

1. To entire new roof the Chancel and both Transepts.
2. To restore the Vaulting under the Central Tower.
3. To remove the present square headed window in the South Transept, and all the debased chancel windows, and substitute new ones.
4. To open the lancet window at present blocked up in the South Side.
5. To remove entirely the Western gallery.
6. To sweep away all the present miserable fittings in the Chancel, and to furnish that and the whole Church with new fittings throughout.

We hope, with the aid of such friends who are willing to assist, to attempt the whole at one. It seems that this Church of all others has a special claim on the liberality of the University and Diocese of Oxford. As having been the residence, ever since the formation of the see, of its Bishops – as being the Church in which the General Ordinations for the Diocese have been already held, and will continue to be held at least in every year; - There seem special reasons why this should be a Model Church for the Diocese, so far as its original construction will admit. At present it cannot be said to be in a condition such as every parish is entitled to.[18]

The cost of the project was to be the princely sum of £2,000. Restoration began with the dilapidated chancel in 1849 under the direction of Benjamin Ferrey: the whole chancel was stripped. Its lathe and plaster roof, mentioned in Parker's guide of 1846,[19] was removed and the memorial tablets to bishops Lloyd and Moss were moved to their present position in the south transept. The small priest's door on the south side (much admired by Parker) was blocked when the substantial oak seating, including a grand bishop's throne, was placed in its present position. New and more fitting windows were added on the north and side sides in which glass was placed containing the coats of arms of many of the Bishops of Oxford from Robert King to Wilberforce. All in all, the chancel gained the appearance of a lofty private chapel dedicated to the bishops of Oxford (an appearance it has retained to the present).

A second phase of restoration began in 1851 and was completed by 1853.

Above 7.7. Wilberforce Coat of Arms in Chancel Window (MC)
Opposite 7.8. Bishop's throne (MC)

7.9. Victorian Chancel window and furnishing (MC)

This time the architect was the recently-appointed diocesan architect, G. E. Street, who built a new groined stone vault over the crossing thereby replacing the seventeenth century ringing gallery. The false ceilings of the transept roofs were also removed to display some fine joists, probably from the seventeenth century. The north transept roof was possibly altered on the west side at this time (although this might date from Bancroft's seventeenth-century restoration): the old roof line is still clearly visible on the tower wall. The square-end pews were retained and treated, with their old poppy heads removed. They were also lowered in accord with the latest Ecclesiological fashions, although the Stuart pews served as a model for the new pews. The whole nave was thereby given its present appearance.

The rectangular south window of the south transept, a relic of Bancroft's 1637 restoration and described by the *Gentleman's Magazine* reporter as 'mean',[20] was removed and the present splayed window, which was deemed more suitable, was inserted. The window above the lancets in the south aisle may also have replaced a seventeenth-century window since there are traces of earlier masonry clearly visible on the outside, although the *Gentleman's Magazine* describes a decorated window. The lancet at the west end of the north aisle replaced a round headed window which, as the same reporter put it, 'from the traces of the repairing about the latter, I suspect it has assumed its present appearance through unskilful craftsmanship'.[21]

New furnishings were made at the same time including an ornate reredos with a large crucifix under which a group of saints was depicted. This was contained within five lancet shaped panels, the three central panels being

7.10. Street's vault in crossing (MC)

7.11. Church in 1821 showing round-headed 'lancet' from *Gentleman's Magazine* xci (1821), frontispiece

taller than the outer two. On each side of the altar a curtain covered the wooden panelling. This elaborate altar was to be the source of some controversy in 1878. The earlier east end, which can just be made out in Hollis's drawing,[22] appears to have been elegantly panelled in typical seventeenth century style with Laudian communion rails. Again this probably dates from Bancroft's restoration. The fine west window glass of Christ in majesty was designed by Street and executed by Hardman in 1852.[23] Less successfully a large and rather ugly stone pulpit with a brass desk was added on the north side in front of the crossing which (thankfully) was removed later in the century.

Pott himself was by all accounts an earnest high churchman. Whilst vicar, he published a collection of sermons preached on Wednesdays at Cuddesdon as part of confirmation preparation and dedicated to Wilberforce. These reveal a typical Victorian piety not dissimilar from that of his dedicatee. At one point he comments on the Church building as having been for hundreds of years 'the place where all holy men who have lived here have drawn nigh to Him that dwells therein, in prayer, in praise in communion … This has been the temple of God to many earnest Christian souls.'[24] Church life at this period was flourishing: the 1854 returns made to Wilberforce on his visitation noted two Sunday

7.12. Church interior with stone pulpit after second restoration (about 1870) (RCC)

7.13. Chancel in about 1900 showing original altar (COS)

services at 11am and 3pm, with sermons at each. There were eighteen communions per year (a very large number for a country parish in those years), held
monthly and on the great feasts, with an average of 70 to 80 at the festivals, and
fifty on a Sunday. Pott comments in a sermon: 'Week by week, Sunday by
Sunday we gather here, to worship, to confess, to be absolved, to pray, to praise,
to hear. Month by month brings round the Communion of the Body and Blood
of our Lord, we come to his table to receive the pledges of his undying love'.[25]
The average Sunday congregation was about 200. On holy days there were
services at 9am and 7pm, with one sermon. It would appear from Pott's sermon
that there were also frequent week-day services, which 'might be resting points
from the trial and labour of the worldly cares of the week, times of refreshing,
and drinking in spiritual strength'.[26] In addition there were about twenty adults
attending church school in winter. These figures were amongst the highest
percentage in the county, and confirmed the returns from the 1851 religious
census, where out of a population of 337, the average Sunday attendance was
about 250.[27] From 1850 Pott was assisted by Henry John Pye, who married the
bishop's daughter, Emily Charlotte in 1851, when he became Rector of Clifton
Campville, Staffordshire. Like Wilberforce's brothers, Henry and Robert, he
seceded to Rome in 1868 and was subsequently called to the Bar in 1876.[28]

Wilberforce's vision and inspired leadership seem to have reaped ample fruit in the village of Cuddesdon. In his diaries, Wilberforce noted (without excessive modesty) after he had he preached at the Morning Service on 2 January 1853: 'A good attendance again, making 125 this Christmas. I trust that there has indeed, of God's goodness, been a marked improvement in the state of this village during the last 7 years.'[29]

Wheatley and the division of the parish

At the same time, Wilberforce set about ensuring proper pastoral provision for Wheatley. It was a village that had long been notorious for its lawlessness, and is said to have been the last place in Southern England where cock-fighting was publicly staged. The curate, Edward Elton, another earnest high churchman, who was to become the first vicar, was concerned by the lack of adequate ecclesiastical care for the village. Although a chapel had been mentioned at Wheatley since the fifteenth century, and Wheatley had also provided one of Cuddesdon's three churchwardens (along with one each from Cuddesdon and Denton), it was still not properly endowed. In addition, there had been uneasy relations between the two main centres of population in the parish for some time: Wheatley may have been the daughter church, but the village was considerably bigger. As already mentioned, the 1630 Court Books of the Bishop of Oxford note that there were difficulties over the collection of payment from Wheatley for seating in Cuddesdon church.

The chapel of ease at Wheatley, which stood where the war memorial now stands, seems to have been quite poor, having only one cope mentioned in the inventory of Edward VI's reign.[30] In 1644 the church was described as having 'no monuments but onely in the East window a picture of St. Nicholas with his armes'. Moves for a better endowment of Wheatley Church were made during the episcopate of Thomas Secker. A letter of 11 January 1745 from Henry Montague pleaded for a substantial increase to the meagre £10 which was given by the bishop to pay a curate to serve Wheatley.[31] In this year, and again in 1749, the living was endowed with £800 partly from Queen Anne's Bounty, the bishop also paying for a curate licensed specifically for Wheatley. Thomas Bray served Wheatley from 1751-85 and was well known as a campaigner against Toryism in the University.

In 1786 a group of well-to-do inhabitants of Wheatley including the churchwarden and the overseers petitioned the bishop for a new church:

> The want of room is such that the principal inhabitants when they have a friend or friends to stay cannot take them to church with them ... every part of it has been falling into decay and ruin ... the roof falling in and

7.14. The short-lived Wheatley Church of 1795 (COS)

7.15. Wheatley Church in 1887 (COS)

the tower in the greatest danger. ... Divine Worship is too often neglected, contrary to the wish of the inhabitants.[32]

The Bishop of Oxford responded positively to the suggestion and a few years later money was forthcoming from the residue of the estate of Thomas Sims of Denton House who had died in 1790. The replacement chapel was being built in 1793, 'a decree in Chancery having been made for that purpose'.[33] It was consecrated on 15 July 1795 and had an immediate effect on religious practice in the village: it was noted in the 1796 visitation that the numbers of Anabaptists had decreased since the consecration of the chapel.[34]

In 1852 the separation of the vicarage of Cuddesdon from the See of Oxford led to a consolidation of the income to the curate with a tithe-rent charge of £208 12s. 9d., and on 15 February 1855 the living of Wheatley was established as a perpetual curacy under the patronage of the Bishop of Oxford.[35] The population of Wheatley was thus no longer forced into the payment of church rates for the upkeep of Cuddesdon church. At about the same time, Elton wrote in his diary on 21 August 1854 of his desire to rebuild the church at Wheatley to replace the eighteenth-century building which Wilberforce described as 'of a hopeless conventicle pattern'. The bishop granted a petition to demolish Wheatley church on 2 December 1855[36] (having first consulted the leading local landowner, the Earl of Macclesfield of Shirburn Castle near Watlington).[37] The bishop felt that Cuddesdon Church could manage adequately without the income from Wheatley. Consequently, Wheatley Church was pulled down in 1856 and replaced with a new church the following year built of Wheatley stone to a bold Early-English design by G. E. Street. Elton managed to raise £3,500 for the construction mainly in small amounts from benefactors in the University. The striking spire was built by Holland of Thame.[38] An old parsonage had existed in Wheatley High Street (now no. 23-25), which by the time Elton was appointed as curate was 'wholly unfit for use' and consequently a new house had to be built which was suitable for the newly-endowed vicar (and which now houses Morland House surgery).[39]

Given the inadequacy of provision for Church of England worship in the eighteenth century, it is not surprising that non-conformity fared better in Wheatley than in Cuddesdon. A Congregationalist church was registered in 1796 and is still thriving as a United Reform Church. In the 1851 census the Chapel attracted approximately 236 against the church's 383.[40] The Granary Hall was acquired by the Plymouth Brethren in 1928. It is currently a Free Evangelical Church with ecumenical relations with the other Wheatley churches.

The Separation of Cuddesdon Vicarage from the See

Following the 1836 Tithe Act the commutation of the Cuddesdon tithe was fixed on 23 June 1840 and based on the 1812 tithe map. The division made meant that the rector was entitled to the tithes of corn and grain which amounted to £145 14s 9*d* and the vicar to the remainder, to the value of £173 10s. 0*d*. plus a further £5 15s. 3*d*. on the glebe.[41] The total titheable land was 986 acres 2 rods and 21 poles, and in addition there were 125 acres, 1 rod and 13 poles which were exempt from tithe. These included The Vent farm in Forest Hill, Pelfrance Farm, King's Arms Close in Wheatley, Rod Eyot fishery on the Thame, Cuddesdon Mill and Holton Wood.[42] In an exchange made by the tithe commissioners between the bishop as vicar and the bishop as rector £3 was awarded for the site of the vicarage, and rectorial tithes amounted to £210 4s. 9*d*. in Cuddesdon and Denton together with a further £19 3s. 2*d*. from other sites. On 15 May 1852 the vicarage of Cuddesdon was separated from the see of Oxford by an Order in Council,[43] which resulted from an act of Parliament severing benefices from sees. The bishop was to hold the advowson. The separation proved a complex piece of legislation because of the need to consolidate the tithe rent charge. Legal opinion was sought from William Dugdale in 1851 who referred to the various settlements of the vicarage and rectory from the fourteenth and seventeenth century.[44] The vicarial tithe income which was transferred to the vicar was £208 12s 9*d*.[45] By 1913 the rent charge in lieu of tithes was £296 17s 7*d*., the gross value being £215 14s. 6*d*. By 1895 the net value of the vicarage was £161, and by 1953 £207.[46] Almost immediately after the establishment of the vicarage the income was used to guarantee £1360 to build a rectory house at Nuneham Courtenay.[47]

Pott succeeded to the Cuddesdon vicarage on its creation and was soon accommodated in a new parsonage house (now called College House) built in 1853-4 in a severe and very ecclesiological style to plans made by G. E. Street dated 12 June 1852. The original house contained a barrel vaulted 'oratory' on the first floor with three lancet windows. It was estimated at £1440. The house proved too small and was enlarged a few years later, with a new oratory added on the ground floor to the left of the front door. The extension rather clumsily concealed the upstairs lancets. This house continued to serve as a vicarage until 1977, although its ownership had been transferred to the College in the 1950s. Since 1977 it has been used solely for College administration, teaching and accommodation.

7.16. The Vicarage (now College House) in 1906 (COS)

The Founding of the College

Wilberforce had further plans for Pott. Christopher Wordsworth (the future Bishop of Lincoln) noted in a letter of 1851:

> It is the Bishop's intention to build and endow a College at Cuddesdon for training candidates for Orders under the Bishop's eye. He intends to combine the superintendence of the College (under himself) with the Incumbency of Cuddesdon of which he is Patron. The Parish Church, which is now a beautiful building, would serve for the Students as a Chapel.[49]

As well as being vicar, clerical secretary to the bishop, and also rural dean of the Cuddesdon deanery, Pott was charged with setting up a new diocesan college for the theological education of graduate candidates for the ministry. 'The offer came upon me suddenly,' Pott later wrote: 'I did not fully realise what the acceptance of such an offer involved, nor how unequal I really was both physically and intellectually for the work. But I did accept it ignorantly.'[50] Pott, who was a modest man and subject to frequent bouts of illness,

Above 7.17. The Opening of the College in 1854 in *Illustrated London News*
Below 7.18. The College in about 1860 (RCC)

became first principal of the new College which opened opposite the Bishop's
Palace on 15 June 1854. Although he was soon overshadowed by the more
ebullient and idiosyncratic vice-principal Henry Liddon, Pott nevertheless
helped set the serious tone for the college, which was soon filled with gradu-
ates of Oxford and Cambridge. Most of the students' time was spent in prayer

7.19. College Reading Room in about 1860 (RCC)

and spiritual reading with the express intention of 'forming character and

moulding habits' of the future clergy of the Church of England.[51]

From that time, the history of the parish church and history of the college have been inseparable, with the principal (and not the vice-principal as *Victoria County History* mistakenly states) remaining vicar until 1996. From its foundation, the college used the church for its evening service, initially only on Wednesdays and Fridays. Students also took part in the 11am Sunday morning service, which was a communion service monthly. On the whole the relationship

7.20. Henry Parry Liddon as Vice-Principal (RCC)

7.21. Archdeacon Pott (RCC)

between church and village was (and remains) good, although at times somewhat strained. An earlier anonymous historian of Cuddesdon church sums it up well (and probably accurately): 'Suffice it to say that the villagers dislike the college, but they hate the man who says anything against it.' Another writer, R. T. Günther, wrote of the quality of the Cuddesdon air as a central part of the priestly formation in a guide book to the Oxford area:

He was a wise man who set the College here, for the breeze blows fresh and keen from the uplands, and they say that those who abide a year here and inhale it go forth again to the world with a right gracious habit and mien:- Pandatur inanes / Suspensi ad ventos.[52]

After some serious difficulties provoked by ritualism in the College, which are well documented by Owen Chadwick,[53] Pott resigned to take up the living of East Hendred in Berkshire. His sermon 'The Parting of Friends', which was probably preached on his departure from Cuddesdon, emphasises the point that 'God's grace is not dependent upon this or that human instrument'.[54] 'In this world,' he goes on, 'change, separation, partings are troublous fruits of the fall: friendships seem to be formed just for a little while and then broken up; relations between priest and people seem to be cemented only that they may be broken down again: it is the condition of this mortal state.'[55] All in all, Pott left a profound mark on Cuddesdon, not least through beautifying and restoring the Church.

Pott was succeeded as vicar and principal on 11 May 1859 by H. H. Swinny, 'a devoted Church of England Christian, sound on the sacraments',[56] possessed, in the words of Wilberforce, of a 'nobleness of spirit which no one who approached him could fail to appreciate: it really seemed as if a low thought could not harbour in his mind'.[57] A more moderate churchman than Pott and Liddon, who had resigned at the same time as Pott, he set the direction for the College which his successor continued. However, he was not destined for long in his post: he was subject to cardiac problems and died on 22 December 1862. He is buried under the yew tree to the north of the church. His son, George Hervey (d. 13 Feb 1887 at Bandawe, Lake

7.22. H. H. Swinny. Second Vicar and Principal (RCC)

Nyasa), and his eldest daughter Louisa Georgina Edith (d. 22 August 1867 at Abbottabad, India), wife of the Revd A. Brinckman, who both served as missionaries, are commemorated in the south-west window with pictures of SS. George and Agnes in the glass, probably by Kempe. It was Swinny's successor who was to make a lasting mark on Cuddesdon and also on the Church of England.

NOTES

1   Marshall, *Diocesan Histories*: Oxford, p. 188.
2   Ashwell, *Life*, i, pp. 309-10. It is reported that an ale-house used to stand in the palace grounds (p. 310). Wilberforce, when visiting before he was bishop, was woken by 'a chorus of yells, howls, shouts &c., like a perfect Jacquerie'. He was informed that this was the 'Garsington men going home from drinking in our ale house'.
3   G. F. A. Best, *Temporal Pillars*, Cambridge: Cambridge University Press, 1964, p. 366.
4   Best, *Temporal Pillars*, p. 366.
5   *Gentleman's Magazine* 26 (December 1846), p. 637.
6   ORO MS Archd. Oxon. b. 23; *Gentleman's Magazine* 27 (Feb 1847), p. 190.
7   Samuel Wilberforce, *Sermons Preached on Various Occasions*, Oxford: Parker, 1877, pp. 79-90, here pp. 88-9.
8   *VCH*, v, p. 101. Life, i, p. 376.
9   *Gentleman's Magazine* 27 (Feb 1847), p. 190.
10   Ashwell, *Life*, iii, p. 408.
11   Ashwell, *Life* i p. 323.
12   Standish Meacham, *Lord Bishop*, Cambridge MA: Harvard University Press, 1970, p.100.
13   H. Kirk-Smith, *William Thomson, Archbishop of York: His Life and Times, 1819-90*, London: SPCK, 1958, p. 5.
14   This freehold of this eighteenth-century house seems to have belonged to the bishop, but probably became the property of the College in 1895 (*Cuddesdon College. A Record and Memorial*, Oxford: Oxford University Press, 1929, p. 31). It was leased to various members of the College staff, often those with dependent relatives. Sometimes it was lived in by students, and sometimes by the curate of the village. It seems to have been sold to Mark Carpenter-Garnier after his retirement as bishop of Colombo, and Michael Ramsey after he retired as Archbishop of Canterbury. It was purchased by Ripon College in 1977 after the amalgamation of Cuddesdon and Ripon Hall.
15   See above Plate 4.7.
16   *VCH*, i, p. 105. MS Top Oxon b.3, ff. 12-16.
17   Minutes of the General Committee, 22 Feb. 1843 cited in W. A. Pantin, 'The Oxford Architectural and Historical Society' in *Oxoniensia*, 4 (1939), pp. 174-94, here p. 178.
18   Proposals for the restoration of Cuddesdon Church (Handbill at Bod. GA Oxon c. 317 (7))
19   Parker, *Guide*, p. 296.
20   *Gentleman's Magazine* xci (1821), pp. 201-2.
21   *Gentleman's Magazine* xci (1821), p. 202.
22   See above Plate 4.7.
23   See above Plate 3.6.
24   *Confirmation Lectures delivered to a Village Congregation in the Diocese of Oxford*, London: Masters, 1852, p. 154.
25   *Confirmation Lectures*, p. 154.
26   *Confirmation Lectures*, p. 155.
27   Kate Tiller (ed.), *Church and Chapel in Oxfordshire*, ORS 55, 1987, p. 30. The population of Cuddesdon (not including Wheatley, Denton and Chippinghurst) was recorded in 1801 as 238; 239 in 1811; 267 in 1821; 317 in 1831; 305 in 1841 and 337 in 1851. Denton increased from 114 to 155 in the same period, and

Chippinghurst decreased from 22 to 13. Wheatley increased in population from 685 to 1037. In 1991 the population of Cuddesdon, Denton and Chippinghurst was 476, a slight decline from the 1851 total.

28   *Letter-Books*, p. 395.

29   Ashwell, *Life*, ii,, p. 157.

30   Rose Graham (ed.), *The Edwardian Inventories for Oxfordshire*, ORS 1, 1919, pp. 65, 127.

31   A. P. Jenkins (ed.), *The Correspondence of Thomas Secker*, ORS 57, 1991, p. 143.

32   Cited in John Fox, *Tanning-Barn to Church. The Dissenting Congregation of Wheatley over Two Hundred Years*, Wheatley URC, 1997, p. 10.

33   ORO ODP, Bishop's Visitation, 1793.

34   ORO Archd. Oxon. c. 327.

35   In 1845 the curate of Wheatley had a stipend of £120. (Ashwell, *Life*, i, p. 381). In 1869 the income of the vicarage was £250.

36   Hassall (ed.), *Records of Wheatley*, p. 98.

37   Letter to the Earl of Macclesfield, 10 Jan 1854: 'We have put our Church here into thoroughly good repair, new roof & c., that for years to come our Church Rate will be most insignificant – and I have every good reason to believe that the rate payers here will agree to set Wheatley free if you as landowner do not object' (*Letter Books* p.296).

38   *VCH*, v, p. 115.

39   Hassall (ed.), *Records of Wheatley*, p. 126.

40   See John Fox, *Tanning-Barn to Church*, p. 27.

41   *VCH*, v, p. 104.

42   By Local Government Order 7,868 of 24 Dec 1878, Vent Farm, Pelfrance and Holton Wood were attached to Holton Parish, and the detached part of the parish in Forest Hill was added to the surrounding parish. See also VCH, v, pp. 115-6.

43   13 & 14 Victoria c. 94 s. 22.

44   4 Henry IV c.12 and 12 Charles I c. 17.

45   The value of the living cited by Ashwell (*Life*, I, p. 381) in 1845 was £440. This compared to £500 for Bray and £294 for Burford. On Wilberforce's translation to Winchester the living was worth £264, compared with £674 for Brightwell and £690 for Middleton Stoney and £34 for Toot Baldon.

46   *VCH*, v, p. 104.

47   ORO ODP c. 1789.

48   ORO ODP c. 1789 (Plan); b. 5 (Estimate).

49   Cited in Owen Chadwick, *The Founding of Cuddesdon*, Oxford: Oxford University Press, 1954, p. 144.

50   Autobiographical memoir (now lost) in Chadwick, *Founding of Cuddesdon*, p.12.

51   Chadwick, *Founding of Cuddesdon*, p. 32.

52   R. T. Günther, *The Oxford Country*, London: John Murray, 1912, p. 48.

53   Chadwick, *Founding of Cuddesdon*. See also Andrew Atherstone, 'The Founding of Cuddesdon: Liddon, ritualism and the forces of reaction' in Mark D. Chapman (ed.), *Ambassadors of Christ*, Aldershot: Ashgate, 2004, ch. 2.

54   Alfred Pott, 'The Parting of friends' in *Village Sermons*, London: Bell and Daldy, 1867, p. 214.

55   'The Parting of friends', p.219.

56   Ashwell, *Life*, ii., p. 367.

57   Chadwick, *Founding of Cuddesdon*, p. 102; *Cuddesdon College. A Record and Memorial*, p. 99.

8.1. Edward King: Third Vicar and Principal (RCC)

Chapter Eight

Edward King and the Later Nineteenth Century

Edward King and Cuddesdon

After a brief interregnum, when Pott assumed temporary responsibility for the College, Edward King, who had been Elton's curate in Wheatley, and who has since been raised to saintly status in the Church of England calendar,[1] succeeded as principal and vicar on 17 April 1863. Although much has been written about his life and work, there is little material on his time as vicar of Cuddesdon. A former curate, writing in G. W. E. Russell's biography, commented that King used to think he did nothing in the parish during his time in Cuddesdon. 'I believe in his answer to the Visitation-question of the Bishop, "What do you find your chief hindrance in parish work?" He used to write as the answer, "The Theological College".' This feeling, which has undoubtedly been shared by subsequent principals, was, however, far from the truth. He devoted Friday nights to seeing people from the parish, and knew them all by name. Most of the farmers were communicants during this time and would send a quantity of their corn to the vicar, out of which the 'Eucharistic loaf' would be baked for the Harvest Festival. King's straightforward preaching was well matched to the peculiarly mixed congregation of farmers, villagers, students and members of the bishop's family.[2]

Another biography relates an episode in King's time at Cuddesdon when, on his forty-second birthday, he was called to visit a man stricken with smallpox. When the man died, so great was the fear of infection that nobody could be found to put the man in his coffin. King placed him in and screwed the lid down, convinced by a premonition that he too would be stricken down by the disease.[3] Such irrationality shocked him: indeed this episode stayed with him until the end of his life as a constant reminder of his human frailty and the power of superstition.

Most of King's memories of the village, however, were happy, and these

8.2. Church in 1870 (with cross) (COS)

too continued to inspire him throughout his ministry. Thirty years after his time in Cuddesdon he wrote to a former student:

> Oh, those Cuddesdon days were very wonderful! I look back on them with unfailing gratitude, though I fear I have fallen below the high aim and hopes we had then. It is hard, sometimes, when people go wrong; but thank God, I believe in the People, and love them down to the ground. I am never happier when I go to the little country parishes, and talk to the dear things.[4]

King enjoyed his time at Cuddesdon and left a lasting mark on the College and village. He undoubtedly took pleasure in the company of the young men, but recognised the inherent dangers in very close friendships between the students and also between the staff and students.[5] His high sense of calling, his understanding of deep friendship, and his evident celibacy make Lord Elton's later speculations about King's homosexuality somewhat implausible.[6] His sanctity, wisdom and understanding were remembered by all who came into contact with him both at Cuddesdon and later in his ministry. Indeed there are few churches in the Diocese of Lincoln which do not still have his picture hanging in the vestry. Canon Henry Scott Holland was later to write of his visits to Cuddesdon in King's time: 'The whole place was alive with him ... He could draw love out of a stone ... All over England there are men who look back to [those days] as to a heavenly vision.'[7] King remained until 1873 when he was appointed first Professor of Pastoral Theology at

8.3. Edward King with the Elton family at Wheatley Vicarage (Private Collection)

Oxford, a post created specifically for him. For the remainder of his life he never lost his love for Cuddesdon. 'My life here,' he said as Bishop of Lincoln at the College Festival in 1900, 'gave me hope of a higher life for myself and a higher life for other people too.'[8]

Cuddesdon in the 1870s and 1880s

During King's time as principal and vicar, John Fielder Mackarness succeeded to the see of Oxford in 1870 after Wilberforce's translation to Winchester the previous year. In 1870 the ancient endowments of the see, including Cuddesdon, were put in the hands of the Ecclesiastical Commissioners in return for an annual stipend of £5,000. This situation continued until 1877 when land from Cuddesdon was attached directly to the see. Mackarness maintained his predecessor's tradition of holding ordination retreats in the palace and of ordaining in Cuddesdon Church at Trinity and Michaelmas.[9] On King's departure Markarness appointed his university friend and fellow high churchman, Charles Wellington Furse as vicar and principal on 26 July 1873. Furse had preached at the bishop's consecration, describing him as 'for thirty-eight years my brother and my friend'.[10] Furse was a married man with a more distinctly partisan understanding of Anglo-

8.4. Church from High Street in 1880s (COS)

Catholicism than his predecessor. He had served his title with the controversial ritualist Father Carter of Clewer, and had become a member of the English Church Union, which had been established to defend ritualist prac-

tices.[11] Edward Francis Willis, his vice-principal, was even more suspect, having been a member of the Society of the Holy Cross, an organisation for mission priests based on Roman Catholic prototypes.

Even though both withdrew from these partisan organisations after they had been appointed to the College, their erstwhile membership was enough to make some (including the veteran controversialist, C. P. Golightly who had instigated the campaign against

8.5. Charles Wellington Furse (RCC)

8.6. Edward Willis (RCC)

the college in the 1850s) suspicious that the college staff were indoctrinating their students with Romanizing practices. Such practices, they held, might well rub off on the ordinary parishioners of Cuddesdon, especially since students were responsible for catechising the children of Cuddesdon on Sunday afternoons.[12] According to Golightly, several farmers had walked out of the parish church when Willis preached there.[13] In the controversy that followed, one of the major local landowners, the Earl of Macclesfield played a prominent role attacking the College. The heated debate focused on the altar in the new college chapel, various ritualist teachings, and secessions to Rome. A handbill of 1878 signed by the Earl notes fifteen 'perverts' who had converted to the Roman Catholic Church.[14] Furse was subjected to a bitter attack from various anti-Ritualist quarters but was defended by many of his former students and also by Bishop Mackarness. The Anglo-Catholic *Church Times*, for instance, called him 'a very moderate, not to say cautious, Anglican churchman'.[15]

At one point in the controversy, the altar in the church had been subject to detailed scrutiny by *The Rock*'s 'special correspondent'. Writing in the staunchly protestant magazine on 13 December 1878 he reported that it was 'of the most repulsive and Popish kind' and he was particularly sickened by one of the figures on the reredos:

8.7. The offending images on the altar (after later restoration) (MC)

It was that of a Pope in full Pontifical garments, and with the unmistakable Papal tiara on his head!!! Therefore when a Ritualistic worshipper bends before the 'altar' in Cuddesdon Church he actually bows before the image of a Pope which a former principal of Cuddesdon has set up![16]

Fortunately, the controversy came to little, both sides claiming victory:[17] the image of the pope (as well as St Jerome in cardinal's hat) still confronts the celebrant at the chancel altar. Nevertheless the controversy did display Mackarness's diplomatic success as a bishop: though sympathetic to high church practices, he strove to steer a course between partisan extremes. It also showed the limits to which a diocesan seminary could go.

Willis resigned in 1879 to become one of the first missionaries of the Oxford Mission to Calcutta, but Furse continued until 1883. Although he was certainly catholic in his leanings he was far from narrowly partisan: he never used eucharistic vestments nor did he attempt to compel the practice of auricular confession on others, even though he practised it himself. He was as concerned as other vicars with administering the church and its building: for instance the gutters were replaced in 1878. Furse was also intricately involved with what went on inside church. He drew up a set of rules for the choir in

8.8. College Chapel in 1880s (RCC)

1882, which display something of the prevailing style of worship. Special attention was called to the following points:

A. Keeping pace with the Minister in those parts of the service which are said together – the Confession, the Lord's Prayer, and Creed.
B. Quietness and smoothness in the confession.
C. Prompt attention to the shorter Responses and Amens.
D. A slight but uniform pause at the colon when monotoning, as well as in chanting the Psalms and Canticles.
E. An erect attitude of the head while kneeling, and not covering the face with the hands.

Most importantly, he went on, 'The choir will remember that the Minister leads the Service, and the Choir is intended to help the people in offering their united worship to the glory of Almighty God.'[18] This rule in particular may not have been easy to enforce.

Furse became archdeacon of Westminster in 1883, dying in August 1900. He is commemorated by a large brass plaque on the north wall of the church. A lychgate was erected in 1877 paid for by members of the College, in memory of his wife, Jane Diana Furse, who tragically died of scarlet fever aged thirty-eight shortly after the birth of a son, leaving her widowed

8.9. Church looking east (1901) (COS)

8.10. The lychgate looking towards the High Street. Postcard (COS)

husband with nine children.[19] Furse's obituarist noted that his 'warm heartedness extended far beyond his family to friends of all classes and kinds'.[20]

William Methuen Gordon Ducat, a 'shrewd, canny Scot, with not a few odd quaintnesses,'[21] who had been chaplain to the College from 1876, succeeded Furse as principal and vicar on 28 Oct 1883. On a more mundane level, this was also the year when insurance premiums began (at £2). Like Pott before him Ducat went on to become Archdeacon of Berkshire. He died on 17 March 1922, and is buried the churchyard beside the main path to the west door. His obituarist wrote that 'No one could be more skilful in reconciling differences of opinion, smoothing down

8.11. Church from west in 1906. Henry Taunt (COS)

differences, and preventing wrangling.'[22] All of these were undoubtedly important characteristics following Furse's somewhat contentious principalship. Ducat's wife was also buried in the churchyard, dying on 24 November 1943, aged 85.

During Ducat's time the Village Reading Room was built in 1886 using funds made available by the Bishop for the 'instruction, recreation and benefit of persons for the time being inhabitants of the said parish of Cuddesdon,' on land made available by the Earl of Macclesfield on a 99 year lease. Two years later, on 14 December 1888, a charity was established using £300 left by the Revd Walter Sneyd to invest 'for the distribution of food and coals amongst the poor of the hamlet of Denton at Christmas in every year' at the discretion of the vicar. This yielded £1 18s. 4*d.* at the beginning, and by 1930 was used to donate 4½ tons of coal to eighteen houses. It still provides a modest income administered with the Child Charity on behalf of the whole parish. It is also important to note that shortly before the end of Mackarness's episcopate a

8.12. Ducat as Vicar and Principal (RCC)

8.13. Bishop Mackarness (RCC)

Wesleyan Chapel was built in 1887 at the Denton Hill end of the High Street. Given the prominence of the Church of England in the village it is hardly surprising that there were so few non-Conformists in Cuddesdon;[23] the Chapel was closed in 1936 and finally pulled down in 1953.

Two Minutes Books survive from Ducat's years:[24] the Bellringers' Association seems to have been set up in 1889. The records noted that 'all fines to be kept in a belfry box', and also that 'the handbell ringers must not ... expect to receive any money at the Palace, Vicarage, or Old Vicarage this Christmas, it being felt that the present system is bad, and must be changed'. These handbells still exist and have recently been renovated. There are also very thorough notes of the celebrations of the Queen's Jubilee on 23 July 1887. Large sums were raised to provide a huge feast for three hundred adults, who were supplied with 450 lbs of meat, 100 lbs of pudding, 1½ sacks of potatoes, seventy five 2 lb loaves of bread, and ¼ cwt of cheese. Two quarts of beer were to be made available to men, and 1 quart for women and 'lads' under eighteen, donated free by both Hall's and Hanley's breweries. There was to be a dry period between 3 and 5.30 when ginger ale would be served at 1*d*. There were 123 men, 121 women and 40 who had left school and were under eighteen. In addition there were 136 children, 110 of whom were on the role of the school.

As well as the feast for the adults there was tea in the afternoon organised by Mrs Mackarness, together with the other wealthy women of the village. A special cake was sent from Boffins of Oxford. At the feast the landowners acted as servers, and Mr J. H. Gale of Dove House organised sports, with various competitive events for all age groups (including a cricket match, and separate races for those in their 30s, and those in their 40s, as well as a wheelbarrow race and egg races). Children were entertained with a sack race, a donkey race and a round-about. The costs were £49. 15s. 2d. against takings of £53 7s. 2d., the bishop having contributed £8, and the vicar £2. The profit was used to buy coal for the poor of the parish. On the great day itself a peel was rung by the bell-ringers, who received an extra pint of beer for their labours. Overall it looked as if all enjoyed the day. Despite the liberal quantities of beer the day seems to have gone off without trouble: only 5s. had to be paid for the policing of the occasion.

8.14. Mackarness window (SS. Peter and Paul) (MC)

In the following year Bishop Mackarness became seriously ill and was forced into retirement in 1888. He died in September the following year. A brass memorial of his coat-of-arms, quartered with the arms of the diocese of Oxford was erected in the chancel. Further brasses and enamels commemorate subsequent bishops until T. B. Strong in 1937. In addition C. E. Kempe designed a memorial window donated in 1891 by clergy who had been associated with Mackarness during his episcopate. It represented SS. Peter and Paul, on whose festival he had been consecrated in 1870 and which was observed for some time as a day of thanksgiving annually in Cuddesdon. The smaller (and less successful) lancet windows were put in at the same time, the gift of the vicar. These showed St John the Baptist preaching, St John the Divine seeing his vision, and some angels.

William Stubbs

William Stubbs, one of the greatest historians of the nineteenth century, succeeded Mackarness as bishop from 1888 to 1901, having been ordained priest in Cuddesdon Church by Wilberforce in 1850. Edward King, who had become Bishop of Lincoln and was at the time embroiled in ritualistic controversies in his diocese, wrote to the new bishop on his translation from Chester: '*I am thankful!* For Cuddesdon and Oxford and for the Province of Canterbury – most thankful. You will love the poor people in the Parish at Cuddesdon, and the College.'[25] King's prediction, however, did not prove true. Stubbs found Cuddesdon an awful burden. He was very retiring, disliked the country, and had a horror of wasting time, finding the constant travel throughout the vast diocese tiresome. He enjoyed plain living and could not justify the expense of the large retinue needed to maintain a country house. His straightforwardness, plain-thinking and matter-of-factness did not seem compatible with the life of a country gentleman enjoyed by his predecessors.

Stubbs unsuccessfully pleaded with the Ecclesiastical Commissioners and the Archbishop of Canterbury to let him sell the palace and to build a house in Oxford. The archbishop (E. W. Benson) responded that Oxford was too near the centre of ecclesiastical controversy. Consequently, he went on (with more than a hint of irony):

> If with the proceeds of the sale of Cuddesdon another house were to be built, Oxford is not the place where it should be set down. And where else? Didcot? Once I spent half a day there. Materially Cuddesdon would in these days fetch nothing – nothing without demesne, and rather less if it had demesne. It is not a country gentleman's place, and seriously I do not believe it would fetch enough money to build a new house with. Meantime, I think its disadvantages exaggerated.

Benson suggested a solution: Stubbs should rent a house in Oxford and let the sick and dying bishop Mackarness live on in the palace. He concluded: 'I do not think it well for Bishops to begin selling church properties'.[26] In the event Stubbs lived in Cuddesdon after Mackarness's death.

Stubbs was never reconciled to Cuddesdon, coming to begrudge every penny that he did not give away; furthermore, he could not tolerate the time spent on triviality. His forthright character meant that he was able to criticise the failings of his predecessor. 'Certainly,' he wrote of his predecessor, Mackarness, in his primary charge of 1890:

> he did all his work well, and he did it himself. He took up what his predecessor [i.e. Wilberforce] had organised, and built upon it; and I

have no hesitation in saying that, by his way of doing the amount of work that Bishop Wilberforce had made imperative on the conscience of his successor, and by that extension and solidification of the work which grew under his hands, he accumulated on his own shoulders a weight of burden which no one man could be expected to sustain with impunity.

Consequently, he asked, 'How is time and strength to be found for this?'[27] For the great academic so much of the bishop's time seemed to be devoted to the mundane. He wrote from Cuddesdon to a friend: 'Life gets weari-

8.15. William Stubbs (RCC)

some sometimes, here at all events where the shortest cessation from work means intolerable *ennui*'.[28] He once lamented on seeing a clergyman's study during a pastoral visit: 'so different from my library at Cuddesdon; but there! What's the use of a study to a man who hasn't time to take a seidlitz powder?'[29] He versified his feeling of Robinson Crusoe isolation in a poem written not long after his move to Cuddesdon:

> I am Bishop of all I survey
> Dean and Chapter don't matter a fig,
> In the central demesne of the See
> I am master of peacock and Pig.
> O Cuddesdon, where can be the charms
> The Commissioners see in thy face?

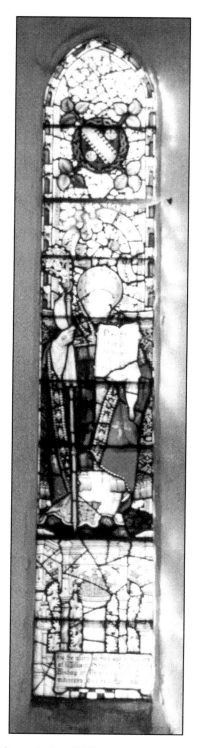

Left 8.17 Bede window (MC) **Right** 8.18 Birinus window (MC)

8.19 Church with new pulpit in about 1900 (COS)

Kettel Hall had been better by far
Than this most inaccessible place.

I am out of the reach of the rail,
I must take all my journeys alone,
There isn't a horse to be hired,
I'm obliged to keep four of my own.
The boy that looks after the beasts
My hat with indifference see,
They don't seem to care in the least
For my Gaiters, or Apron, or me.

O Oxford, O Chester, and Town,
O Bodley, S. Paul's and Roodee,
O had I the wings of a dove
I know where I'd willingly be.
My sorrows I then might assuage
With a leisurely stroll in the Rows,
I'd endure a Beethoven in 'C,'
I'd wear unprofessional clothes.

Though I do not complain of the work,
And silence is good for a change,
I like to be able to shirk
The functions I feel to be strange.
But the sound of the church-going bell
Is the only sweet note that I hear;
I might like the tone very well
Were it not so confoundedly near.

The winds that have borne me aloft
Up here with the pigeons and rooks,
Convey me a kindly review
Of some of my lectures and books.
My friends on the Council may send
Me a vote of regret by decree,
Or the men that were passed in the schools,
Who might have been plucked but for me.

How slow is the Great Western train
As it crawls up by Wycombe to Town![30]
It is hard work enough to get up,
It is harder work still to get down.
When the milk-cans are fairly on board
For a moment I seem to be there,
But they only are shunting the train,
And I find that we are where we were.

But the ring-dove has gone to its nest,
The Peacock is up in his tree,
I'm afraid that I can get no rest –
They'll be cooing and squawking by three.
But to cry over milk that is spilt
Is a weakness I cannot endure,
We must e'en make the best of a lot
Which only Translation can cure.

Stubbs may never have come to enjoy life in the country, but he chose to be buried in the churchyard. He is also is remembered in the church by the communion rails in the chancel as well as the two windows in the lancets at the west end of both aisles, which portray the venerable Bede, a great fellow historian, and Birinus, the missionary responsible for establishing Christianity in Oxfordshire. Stubbs died in Cuddesdon on 22 April 1901, and was buried three days later by the path that leads from the palace to the church. His wife, Catherine, who died in 1942, aged 103, was buried with him. His daughter Katherine, who died in 1939, is also buried in the churchyard. She was responsible for carving the wooden pulpit designed by Kempe in 1895 which was placed on the south side of the chancel arch in 1896 with the loss of two sittings. Although not particularly distinguished, it is a definite improvement on the stone pulpit which was part of Street's restoration.

NOTES

1   His feast day kept on 4 March.
2   G. W. E. Russell, *Edward King*, London: Smith, Elder, 1912, pp. 31-2
3   B. W. Randolph and J. W. Townroe, *The Mind and Work of Bishop King*, London: Mowbray, 1918, p. 55.
4   Russell, *Edward King*, pp. 30-32.
5   In answer to Lord Elton's accusations, see the balanced account in John A. Newton, *Search for a Saint: Edward King*, London: Epworth, 1977, pp. 45-8.
6   Lord Elton, *Edward King and Our Times*, London: Geoffrey Bles, 1958, p. 52.
7   Henry Scott Holland, *A Bundle of Memories*, London: Wells Gardner, Darton & Co., 1915, p.51.
8   *Cuddesdon College, Record and Memorial*, 1904, p. 52.
9   Charles Coleridge Mackarness, *Memorials of the episcopate of John Fielder Mackarness, D.D., Bishop of Oxford*, Oxford: Parker, 1892, pp. 47-51.
10 C. W. Furse, *Command by Sympathy, A Sermon*, London, 1870, p. 15.
11 A flavour of Furse's earnest High Churchmanship can be gained from C. W. Furse, *The Beauty of Holiness: Meditations and Addresses*, London: John Murray, 1903. On Furse, see Michael Furse, *Stand Therefore! A Bishop's Testimony of Faith in the Church of England*, London: SPCK, 1953, Chapter 1.
12 Furse, *Cuddesdon College. A Report to the Bishop of Oxford*, Oxford, 1878, p.9. Cited in Andrew Atherstone, 'Charles Golightly (1807-1885), Church Parties and University Politics in Victorian Oxford', Oxford D. Phil. Thesis, 2000, Chapter 8.
13 Golightly, *A Solemn Warning against Cuddesdon College*, Oxford (privately printed), 1878, p. 5. Cited in Atherstone, 'Charles Golightly'.
14 Bod. G.A. Oxon c. 317. A similar outcry was published in the special *Oxford Times* edition for the Diocesan Conference on 21 Dec 1878, p. 1. Cited in Atherstone, 'Charles Golightly'.
15 *Church Times*, 13 December 1878, p. 706.
16 *The Rock*, 13 December 1878, p. 997. The pope in question is Gregory the Great. Cited in Atherstone, 'Charles Golightly', p. 260.
17 *The Guardian*, 24 December 1878, p. 1793.
18 *All Saints' Church Choir Rules*, printed privately in 1882 (in Bodleian Library).
19 A cover to a chalice was also donated in memory of Furse in 1882 (1913 terrier).
20 *The Guardian*, 15 August 1900, p. 1148.
21 *Record and Memorial*, 1904, p. 115.
22 *The Guardian*, 24 March 1922, p. 214.

23   The 1851 census noted that there were no dissenters in Cuddesdon. See Kate Tiller (ed.), *Church and Chapel in Oxfordshire*, p. 30.

24   ORO CPR d.2.

25   W. H. Hutton, *Letters of William Stubbs, Bishop of Oxford*, London: Constable, 1904, p. 174.

26   Hutton, *Letters of William Stubbs*, pp. 177-8.

27   William Stubbs, *A Charge delivered to the Clergy and Churchwardens of the Diocese*, Oxford: Oxford University Press, June 1890, p. 11.

28   Hutton, *Letters of William Stubbs*, p. 180.

29   Hutton, *Letters of William Stubbs*, p. 182. Wilberforce also commented on Cuddesdon's isolation later on in his episcopate: in his diary on 31 July 1861 he remarked: 'how solemn and awful in its loneliness' (Ashwell, *Life*, iii, p. 18).

30   On the Wheatley Railway, which was built between 1862-4 and opened on 24 October 1864, see Fox (ed.), *One More Millennium*, pp. 40-44.

Chapter Nine

The Twentieth Century to the Second World War

From Johnston and Paget to the First World War

After Ducat's resignation, Stubbs appointed John Octavius Johnston as principal and vicar in January 1895. Shortly after his arrival repairs had to be made to the chancel. Such repairs were traditionally a responsibility of the rector, which in Cuddesdon's case had been the bishop. Given that the bishop, through the ecclesiastical commissioners, was still in receipt of the rectorial tithe rent charge of £325 from the tithe award of 1840, then it was possible to make a case for his liability. The diocesan registrar (Davenport) and Alfred Pott, the former vicar, and now Archdeacon of Berkshire, decided that the 'liability to repair the chancel must rest with the Vicar of Cuddesdon, and the bishop and ecclesiastical commissioners are absolved from the liability'. It was decided that the rectory had been completely suppressed under an order in council and all remaining rectorial lands had been acquired by the college.[1] E. E. Holmes wrote to Johnston on 21 June 1896: 'roughly speaking the above conclusions look conclusive! Cheering for the vicar'. Pott, however, disagreed: 'I believe myself that the Bishop is still Rector, although he holds vicarial property and not the great tithes. The question of chancel repairs never arose in my time, because the church having been restored throughout no repairs were needed.' Eventually the Commissioners paid £8 5s. 0d. but admitted no further liability for chancel repairs.[2]

Church finance was proving more difficult after the abolition of the church rate: in 1865, the income still amounted to £77 15s. 4½d., whereas when the 'voluntary' rate was introduced, it yielded a mere £13 12s. 8d. in 1895. Ad hoc fundraising campaigns had to be organised, although wealthy landowners and the bishop continued to be major benefactors. Lord Macclesfield, who owned much of the land at this time, contributed £3 annually. When a new heating system was purchased in 1896, the college contributed over £5 1s. 10d. and when major repairs were required on the fabric in 1902, the bishop's

9.1. John Octavius Johnston (RCC)

executors paid £10 and the vicar £10.

Seven years after Johnston's appointment, Francis Paget succeeded Stubbs as Bishop of Oxford from 1902. He was the first Bishop of Oxford to have been trained at the College and felt little of his predecessor's isolation, resuming Wilberforce's custom of pre-ordination retreats in the Palace before his Trinity ordinations in the parish church. He was also the first bishop to own a motor car which allowed him great liberty to tour the vast diocese. Although he died at Cuddesdon, his body was taken to Oxford for burial in the Cathedral.[3] It was noted by Dr Hassall that Paget was never 'too busy to take an interest in the village'.[4]

Not long after Paget had become bishop a double tragedy happened near Cuddesdon Mill on 27 June 1903. A tablet on the west wall of the tower staircase records the death of the Revd E. T. Pinson, who shortly beforehand had become curate of the parish and Hebrew lecturer at the college, and who had drowned attempting to prevent one of his choirboys from drowning in the River Thame. In the event the boy died as well. Paget himself composed the inscription:

In loving memory of Alan John Martin, a Chorister of this Church, and of Edward Thomas Pinson, Curate of this Parish, who did not fear to face death as he tried to save a lad's life. They died together in the waters of the Thame: their bodies lie in one grave near this Church: and with one sorrow and one hope for them their friends in Cuddesdon set this record here, Anno Dni, 1903. He sent from on high, He took me, He drew me out of many waters.[5]

The curate and the boy are buried together in a single grave on the north side of the main path leading up to the church.

The remainder of Johnston's years seem to have been happier and the parish thrived. He was a relatively austere high churchman as might be expected from the biographer and devoted disciple of Henry Liddon, the first vice-principal of the College (whose literary executor was Bishop Paget). Nevertheless he sought to ensure that Cuddesdon men were not too partisan in their leanings.[6] He was to become the longest serving vicar and principal and was responsible for a major

9.2. Francis Paget (RCC)

addition of the college, the wing known now as Rashdall, after the Modernist and unorthodox Dean of Carlisle and benefactor of Ripon Hall. It was previously known as King, after the saintly and orthodox Bishop of Lincoln. During Johnston's time, Cuddesdon men had gradually begun to fill many important posts both in England and throughout the Empire. Every other year a grand festival was held in the church with a procession through the village at which a major ecclesiastical dignitary would praise the merits of Cuddesdon's special brand of inoffensive high churchmanship, as well as its rural tranquillity. Archbishop Cosmo Gordon Lang (the first Cuddesdon-trained man to become Archbishop of York and then of Canterbury), for instance, preached in the Parish Church at the 1911 festival:

> We meet to-day as brothers, sharing and renewing the happy memories of home. By you, as for me, this dear Cuddesdon, with its Chapel, its Parish Church, its fields and trees, its long vistas of hills and plains

9.3. Cuddesdon Palace in 1906 (from Church Tower) (COS)

stretching before us this day in all their quiet splendour, is ever cherished as the true home of our ministry.[7]

Such eulogising has not been unusual throughout the history of the College. Lang retained an extraordinary affection for Cuddesdon, writing to his parents shortly after his ordination:

It was not, as you imagined, in Christ Church Cathedral, but in Cuddesdon Church – in my own spiritual Home – my true birthplace – the centre of the highest and deepest associations of my life. Was it not a sign of the goodness of our Father that He so ordained?[8]

The service registers survive from 1910 and reveal a great deal of activity in the church: there were regular weekday communions, and on Sundays the usual pattern consisted of communions at 7am and 8am, matins at 11am (with a monthly sung eucharist), a children's service at 2.30pm and evensong at 6.30pm. Easter communicants before the First World War averaged about 130. Many clergy who went on to be famous visited the church: on 15 September 1912, for instance, William Temple preached. The terrier (inventory) of 1913 indicates something of the style of worship: there were 17 single-breasted cassocks (presumably for the choir who were singing from the *Cathedral Psalter* and *Hymns Ancient and Modern*), as well as eleven stoles in all colours, which reveals ritualistic tendencies, as does the use of the word 'missal' to indicate the three service books (all of which were Books of Common Prayer). Readings came from a

9.4. Charles Gore (RCC)

large Authorised Version as well as a Revised Version. The church was already supplied with electricity in 1913, presumably from the college generator, with thirty-one hanging pendant lamps.[9]

Bishop Paget died in 1911, having celebrated at the 8am service the Sunday before his death. Expressing late Victorian taste, he had redecorated the palace with William Morris wallpapers; these tastes, it seems, were not shared by his successor, Charles Gore, who had earlier been vice-principal of the College under Furse, succeeding Willis in 1879 and who had gone from the College to become first Principal of Pusey House.[10] An aristocratic and socialist ascetic with a liking for nature and the simple pleasures, Gore greatly enjoyed living in the palace, finding the garden in particular an unending joy. Indeed he found Cuddesdon more to his taste than episcopacy. He thought some of the pomps of his position quite ludicrous, even refusing to wear his gaiters at home (a radical statement in those days). Despite having previously served at Worcester and Birmingham, he later wrote: 'I hated being a bishop. How I hated being a bishop! But it had its compensations, primarily the kitchen garden at Cuddesdon, where my admirable gardener kept me in green peas from May until October.'[11] As Bishop of Oxford, Gore fraternised with the students, allowing them to use his garden for recreation. He entertained frequently and there was a constant stream of people to Cuddesdon, including his trusted theological colleagues in the Holy Party, who had earlier produced the controversial ground-breaking manifesto of liberal Anglo-Catholicism, *Lux Mundi* of 1889. During the First World War, as his part in the war effort, Gore asked his gardener to dig up the lawn to plant potatoes. When the crop turned out to be poor he consoled himself by observing the many different species of birds that visited.

It was also during the War that Gore's closest friend and confidant, Henry Scott Holland, a member of the Holy Party who became a canon of St Paul's and was well-known as a great preacher and Christian Socialist (and author of a popular piece 'Death is nothing at all' often read out at funerals)[12] was buried in the churchyard in March 1918. Scott Holland, who had been ordained in Cuddesdon church, had a particularly strong affection towards the village. At a College Festival he spoke eloquently of this affection, something shared by many clergy:

> This is the beginning; and ah! which of us does not know by what sweet entanglements Cuddesdon threw its net about our willing feet? Some summer Sunday, perhaps, we wandered here, in undergraduate days, to see a friend; and from that hour the charm was at work. How joyous, how enticing the welcome, the glad brotherhood! So warm and loving it all seemed, so we thought, of the sharp skirmishing of our talk in college; so buoyant and rich, as we recalled the thinness of our Oxford interests. The little rooms like college-rooms just shrinking into cells, the long talk on the summer lawn. The old church with its quiet country look of patient peace, the glow of the evening chapel, the run down the hill, under the stars, with the sound of Compline Psalms still ringing in our hearts – ah happy, happy day!
>
> It was enough. The resolve that lay half slumbering in our souls took shape, it leapt out. We would come to Cuddesdon when the time of preparation should draw on. ... here, where every stone of the church, every voice in our ear, every memory in the soul, speak of the mercy and goodness of a Master whose companions fail not, but are new every morning ... Oh that we may go from Cuddesdon hill, every one of us, today, strong in the renewed communion of which our very denials have taught us to measure the true strength: go back with the voice of the Lord in our souls, re-enacting its choice, reasserting its desire that in Him alone, and by Him alone, we should set ourselves to find his flock and his sheep.[13]

9.5. Cuddesdon Palace in about 1910. Postcard (COS)

On another occasion, when he was being driven out from Christ Church for the College Festival, the car stopped at the junction at the top of Horspath hill. Scott Holland looked out over the hills. As a large flight of starlings flew over their heads he said: 'How like the Church of England! Nothing apparently keeping it together; and yet somehow getting along all the time. Dear little Anglican birds.'[14] His grave lies to the north-west of the church, a few yards north of where the path divides.

The First World War and the 1920s

Johnston resigned as Principal and vicar in December 1913 becoming Chancellor of Lincoln cathedral. He died on 6 Nov 1923 and was buried in Cuddesdon churchyard with a memorial stone paid for by his old students.[15] He was succeeded in February 1914 by James Buchanan (Jimmy) Seaton, Archdeacon of Johannesburg and previously Vice-principal of Leeds Clergy School. The outbreak of the First World War shortly after his appointment meant that the College's activities were severely curtailed and later, in the climate of post-war reconstruction, many of its more severe rules were quietly allowed to be forgotten. Indeed, with Johnston's departure and the First World War, the continuity with the founders of the College had been broken.

During the War there were significant changes in church government which led to the introduction of the Church Assembly and Parochial Church Councils following the Enabling Act of 1919. This resulted in greater lay

9.6. James Buchanan Seaton as Bishop of Wakefield (RCC)

participation in decision-making processes. Cuddesdon set up a provisional council before the legislation had been passed by parliament. This met for the first time on 26 May 1917. The pattern for future agendas was set at this meeting which concentrated on reducing expenditure and complaining about the amount that was to be paid to central diocesan funds, the diocesan 'quota' (£8). Funds were also raised for the work of the Church Army in France.[16] By 1921 the quota had risen to £16. The first meeting of the PCC proper, which decided to limit numbers to twelve, took place on 23 December 1919.

The first electoral roll consisted of 221 names.[17]

In 1918 it was announced that a friend of the vicar's, Stuart Johnson, had offered to present a 'war shrine' to the church which would contain the names of those who had lived or worked in Cuddesdon, including members of the college.[18] Seaton made the suggestion that the village cross be restored and set up as a memorial,[19] although in the end a very modest wooden crucifix flanked by panels on either side was placed at the easternmost end of the north aisle, backed by a curtain. According to the next vicar, Eric Graham 'The result was a poor affair'. It was later moved to the north-west aisle wall. A more impressive memorial was erected in the front quadrangle of the College. The war was also remembered in the church by the memorial to John Hugh Gale of the Royal Flying Corps erected in 1917. A new clock, which replaced its eighteenth century predecessor, was dedicated to the memory of Alfred James Usborne, nephew of Sir Edward O'Malley of Denton House, on St James's day in 1919.

After much discussion in the new PCC, plans were made to fit out the south transept as a chapel and to reconstruct the chancel. There were also

9.7. War Shrine (COS)

suggestions to remove the vestry from the south porch and relocate it in the north transept, and also to move the organ to a west gallery.[20] In 1921 the high altar was reconstructed and considerably enlarged to designs by F. G. Howard in the latest 'English' fashion with riddle posts and curtains. Such a style appealed to the College's decided English catholic tendencies against the Romanizing trends prevalent in other quarters. The reredos was redesigned using panels from the ugly Victorian original, but retaining the cardinal's hat and papal tiara which had so offended the *Rock's* correspondent in 1878. It was agreed in 1919 to replace *Hymns Ancient and Modern* with the *English Hymnal*, which was equipped with hymns for every eventuality in English catholic worship.[21] There were also changes to the timings of services: a 10am sung eucharist was introduced most Sundays which gradually displaced the 11am matins as the main Sunday service, and which reflected changing ecclesiastical taste.[22] In 1927 there was a PCC motion approving of the deposited prayer book (which was later rejected by Parliament).[23]

Parochial life in the 1920s carried on much as before, although fund raising was becoming more important than before the war. At Christmas 1921 there were 101 communicants out of a population of 322.[24] The vicar expressed his anxiety about the low numbers of young men attending church and asked members of the PCC to do all they could to improve the situation.[25] There was an active team of bellringers, which went on regular outings,[26] and there was briefly a Girl Guides Company at the beginning of the decade. Church

9.8. Chancel with reconstructed altar (COS)

funds were growing increasingly short: although the voluntary church rate continued, it was proving difficult to collect, which meant that a fete was held in the Bishop's gardens in the summer.[27] In 1928, shortly before his departure, Seaton reported to the PCC that the students were keen on giving a Morris Dancing display to the village, which occurred early in the summer in the vicarage garden.[28] In the end, this proved to be the rather bizarre final event of Seaton's long incumbency, and he left the rural idyll of Cuddesdon after serving some fourteen years, to become bishop of the industrial diocese of Wakefield in 1928. He died on 25 May 1938.

Hubert Burge succeeded as Bishop of Oxford on Charles Gore's resignation in 1919. Burge was a typical establishment figure having been headmaster of Winchester College and Bishop of Southwark from 1911. A somewhat less memorable figure than his predecessor, he too seems to have warmed to life in Cuddesdon, enjoying the relaxation of the country as well as the proximity of the College. As Bishop of Southwark, he looked

9.9. Bishop Hubert Burge (RCC)

forward to future country walks, writing to a friend shortly before his translation to Oxford: 'I do believe I shall tempt you to come to me at Cuddesdon and go for a walk over Shotover – that's a treat to look forward to.'[29] He was a regular celebrant in Church. He died in 1925 after only six years as bishop and was buried in the churchyard.

Thomas Banks Strong followed Burge as Bishop of Oxford in 1925. A man of eccentric habits, he refused to make any concessions to the modern fads of pastoral sensitivity or ecclesiastical nicety. A former Dean of Christ Church with a reputation for absolute punctuality and with a razor-sharp wit, he found much in his new role quite insufferable. He was an able musician and had become used to a high standard of music at Christ Church. He once remarked that the sound produced by a village choir 'was such as to twist the intestines of a hyena'. On other visits around his predominantly rural diocese he often insisted on playing the organ himself, and he regularly played in Cuddesdon Church. At one point, so loathsome did he find the noise that he asked for the Cuddesdon church bells to be silenced: the belfry is still blocked in the direction of the Bishop's Palace. As a bachelor he found the village of

9.10. T. B. Strong (RCC)

Cuddesdon rather too rural and remote, but he was intimately involved with every aspect of college life. His main act of generosity to the village was to open up his gardens on Good Friday to allow the children to pick flowers for the Easter posies. An old-fashioned high churchman, he hated dressing up and on one Easter Sunday he reluctantly conceded to wear a cope in procession from Cuddesdon church. He wrote to the then vicar, Eric Graham, 'Hoping I shall not fall down or put my foot through the cope. I remain, etc.'[30] To the end of his life he retained a quill pen and an utter distaste for anything that smacked of enthusiasm. In the brief note about the sale of the Bishop's House in 1978 in the Oxford Times Strong was remembered as 'greatly loved. … There are many who still recall the simplicities of his bachelor household, presided over by a dour and formidable manservant.'[31]

Eric Graham and the 1930s

At Strong's suggestion Eric Graham, who was vicar of Boyton with Sherrington, Wiltshire, having previously been Vice-principal of Salisbury Theological College, was presented to the living by the Lord Chancellor, who was presumably exercising the right of presentation on behalf of the bishop. He was inducted in January 1929. The bishop despised those who sought to follow in the steps of their sainted predecessors and was impressed by Graham's independence of mind. There was a close friendship between the two men: Strong was particularly keen that the College should resist the temptations towards ritualism which were at their height in the 1920s and that it should retain its broad nature.[32] During Graham's time, Archbishop Lang came regularly to take retreats for the students on what he called his 'annual soul-cure in my holy place'.[33]

Like his sainted predecessor, Edward King, Graham found it difficult to balance his commitments as principal and vicar. The normal solution to this problem had been to appoint a curate, but curates were also usually officers of the College which meant that they too had competing priorities. In November 1936 he approached Strong with a view to separating the offices of vicar and prin-

9.11. Eric Graham as Bishop of Brechin seated in College Chapel. Oil Painting (RCC)

cipal. The bishop responded by pointing out that if the College had its own services then the arrangement might work, but any other scheme might well have difficulties. If the principal and vicar did not work together, however, there could be a 'very serious mess'.[34] Strong felt the only possible change would have to be a complete separation of the parish and College. Graham responded with a suggestion to the bishop that the bishop himself should be incumbent (an interesting return to the situation before 1852). Strong replied (correctly in view of the changes in the law in the 1840s): 'I do not think the Bishop can legally be incumbent of a parish. If he holds any parish, when he is consecrated it becomes vacant ... it would of course be possible to appoint someone as Vicar who was not Principal.'

While the difficulties of the dual role were probably mainly a figment of Graham's imagination, they were perhaps also partly a response to the perception of the College by the village: there was always the feeling that it was neglected by the clergy in favour of the young men in training. And there may well have been something more personal: Graham was a shy man with little small talk and a formal manner which did not endear him to some in the parish. He was, however, a fine cricketer which endeared him to others. He was seldom seen out of clerical dress, even on the most informal of occasions, and he seems to have introduced a number of distinctly ritualist practices to the parish including processions at evensong from Easter 1931. It is reported that he was always in church at least half an hour before the service. Every week there was a procession from the vestry of all the robed clergy. His biographer, Holtby, put it discreetly: 'He was not a solemn person, but his manifest seriousness of purpose, together with his other characteristics, and a wit more likely to be appreciated in academic than rural circles, hindered the achievement of spontaneous relations with his people.'[35] He concluded: 'Respect, even (in some) reverence; admiration, even affection; but not popularity: such was the feeling of the parish for its Principal-Vicar.' An interesting example of Graham's wit is related by E. J. K. Roberts, vice principal in 1936, and a beekeeper who went on to become Bishop of Ely. After he had asked whether it might be possible to listen to the King's abdication speech after Compline, Graham replied: 'The Vice has arranged for a wireless set to be placed in the Common Room after Compline ... as is our custom at Cuddesdon when Kings abdicate'.[36]

Re-ordering the church

Another possible source of friction in the 1930s was the re-ordering of the church building which can always be a fraught subject with PCCs. Graham's liturgical sense meant that he was particularly keen on re-ordering the church. Shortly after his appointment he announced that he did not like the dimensions of the high altar and wished to have them changed.[37] Early the following year he had managed to obtain an anonymous donation of £50[38] and set about arranging for plans to be drawn up by the architect, H. S. Rogers, who had designed the War Memorial at Oriel College. Graham announced that another £150 had been given by the same donor, but when the plans were eventually received they were costed at £400.[39] Another £200 was given and in 1931 the alterations were carried out:[40] the sanctuary step was expanded to make the sanctuary more spacious and the altar was rebuilt. It was eventually revealed that the donor was Harold Montagu Hyde-Lees. The altar was dedicated on 30 April 1933.[41]

The south transept (popularly referred to as the 'Well') was also partially converted in 1931 into a Lady Chapel in memory of Principal Ducat with a stone altar built into the blind arch and with a curtain hung behind, made possible by a gift of £100 from Mrs Ducat.[42] This funded the altar stone and its props, the frontal and the dossal. Thereafter the chapel was used regularly

9.12. The High Altar after Graham's extension (MC)

for the weekday services in the vacations, though plans for reseating it were never carried out.[43] There were some thoughts later in the 1930s about beautifying the altar with communion rails and an oil painting, which was suggested by H. S. Rogers.[44] Rogers's drawing reveals a taste for the baroque.[45]

At the dedication of the new altar on All Saints' Day, 1931, the service consisted of 'Mattins and Holy Eucharist', a pattern which had developed into the main Sunday Service at the end of the 1920s. Extra prayers from the 1928 Prayer Book (which had been rejected by Parliament but which was sanctioned for use by the diocesan bishops) were added to the Communion Service from 1930. Graham expressed his frustration with the whole process of liturgical reform, even calling for disestablishment of the Church of England at a PCC meeting.[46] During the 1930s Holy Week was celebrated with great solemnity by the College with many villagers also attending the Holy Week retreat: on Palm Sunday 1939 it was noted that 100 Palms were not enough. The feast-day services during the vacations, most notably Christmas, were rather less grand: no midnight communion was held before the Second World War and Christmas communicants numbered fewer than sixty. Numbers on the electoral roll had also declined significantly to an average of about 180 through the 1930s.

Shortly after the rebuilding of the sanctuary the pipe organ was removed

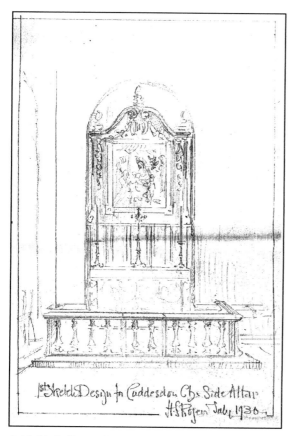

¹ˢᵗ Sketch Design fr Cuddesdon Chʳ Side Altar

HS Rogers July 1930

9.13. H. S. Rogers's Design for South Transept Altar (ORO)

from the north transept. The north end of the north transept was converted into a vestry with proper cupboards and a chest for the vestments. In addition Graham provided a washstand with an element and a plug, as well as a bell-rope in the transept for ringing bells during the celebration, both of which have now disappeared. This made possible the removal of the vestry from the south porch, which had been mentioned by Ducat in his sermon of 1887,[47] and which once again became a doorway, allowing a marginally more sheltered entry into the church. At some stage choir stalls had been placed in the crossing which to Graham's mind seemed cluttered and which he was determined to remove. He noted: 'The preliminary steps were made easy by a piece of luck: the necessity of repairing a break in the east wall of the sanctuary. This meant that the altar had to be moved temporarily', the obvious place being under the tower. This required the removal of some of the offending stalls. Not long afterwards the remainder were removed. Graham remarked: 'I cherished the hope that they would never be replaced'; his hope was realised and they never were.[48]

Changes in liturgical practice led to further re-ordering of the church later in the 1930s. With the rise of the sung communion as the main Sunday service the need for a visible altar was paramount. Plans to this end were executed by Stephen E. Dykes-Bower, 'not then an eminent person' with a new altar to be positioned in the crossing under the tower. After a Faculty dated 12 July 1940 these alterations, which were estimated at £340, were begun in 1941 with the removal of the two front pews from the east end of the

9.14. The Transept Altar as Constructed (COS)

9.15. Church with choir stools before screen and crossing altar in *Record and Memorial*

9.16. Dykes-Bower's Plans of 1940 (RCC)

nave, as well as one from the east end of the north aisle. The crossing floor was raised and tiled, and a large wrought-iron screen was constructed at the entrance to the chancel behind the new altar which effectively created a separate church of the chancel which had the appearance of the bishop of Oxford's private chapel. An aumbry was constructed at the same time in the north wall of the sanctuary. Work was accomplished as a memorial to John Freeman Russell,[49] who had been vice-principal of the College from 1928-1934 living with his mother at the Old Vicarage. He had died shortly after leaving Cuddesdon as dean of Oriel in 1937 aged 39 and is buried in the churchyard. Graham wrote of him: 'To those who shared his life at Cuddesdon, his very presence was a daily benediction; and it is impossible to forget either the profound humility and reverence which marked his celebration of the Holy Mysteries, or the sermons which he preached in the parish Church; flawless gems of spiritual insight.'[50]

This would have made way for the next stage of the restoration. Dykes Bowers' plans and drawings show iron screens with small gates at the west end at the entry to both transepts from the crossing.[51] Another drawing shows a red carpet underneath the altar.[52] The south transept was also to have been fitted as a Lady Chapel with wooden panelling to the level of the monuments. It was also to have contained wooden seating positioned on the stone seats with permanent kneeling desks. The plans also show that two pews were to have been removed from the east end of the south aisle. A portable oak kneeler was to have been made to be positioned in front of the crossing during

9.17. Dykes-Bower's Drawing of Proposed
screen to South Transept (ORO)

communion and to be kept in the space vacated by the removal of the pews when not in use. None of these plans was executed, with the effect that the south transept has become home to an ugly fuse box and a strange and now redundant altar.

In place of the pipe organ a Hammond organ was presented by Boosey and Hawkes, a gift made through 'episcopal and other old students'. Holtby remarks that Graham 'accepted the fact that Cuddesdon Church had gained considerably from the advertisement value of a gift the merits of which (it was supposed) would be evident to generations of men who themselves were to become parish priests.'[53] This plan probably failed to achieve many sales for Hammond organs: recordings made of the College Centenary service in 1954 indicate its inadequacy as an instrument. Rogers also provided plans for an organ case in the north aisle, again with baroque flourishes and gilding in May 1933, and in 1937 Dykes Bower made drawings for a fine west gallery with a grand organ case to be placed directly above the west door,[54] presumably in the place where the earlier gallery had stood in the nineteenth century. Curly pillars based on the south porch of the University Church in Oxford were to support it. Again the war intervened before work could be carried out (probably thankfully).

In May 1939 the Bishop's Palace and the College had been placed on the register of buildings to be requisitioned in time of War. The Principal was forced to leave the vicarage which was required to house the remaining students, and he moved with his wife and six children to the Old Vicarage. Parish and College activity declined quickly with Easter Communicants dropping to a mere 61 by 1942. This was despite the presence of Cosmo Gordon Lang, who had recently retired as Archbishop of Canterbury and who signed the service register 'Lang of Lambeth' with a note to the effect that this was the first time he had used this signature.[55] Shortly after this, however, there was an event which rebounded badly on the College and principal and which further increased tensions with the village. The vice-principal, Geoffrey Walmsley and Chaplain, Francis Etherington, both seceded to the Roman Catholic Church. This was a delicate issue for a number of years. When Graham left to become Bishop of Brechin in 1944, there were moves in the parish to separate the offices of principal and vicar, which Kenneth Riches, the next holder of the offices, firmly resisted.

9.18. The Chancel Gate (MC)

Bishop Kenneth Kirk and the 'problem of Cuddesdon'

During Graham's period as vicar the relationship between the bishop and the village changed fundamentally. After Strong resigned the bishopric in 1937 he was succeeded by another Oxford don, Kenneth Kirk, a serious-minded moral theologian. A man somewhat less puckish in manner and a more 'modern' and managerially-inclined bishop than his predecessor, he found Wilberforce's extensions to the Jacobean Palace quite unsuited to the tasks of a twentieth-century bishop. If the house was to be retained at all, he thought, it should be reduced in size and used solely as a private residence. He explained his intentions to the Diocesan Conference shortly after his consecration:

My plans have been shaped to a very large extent by what I may call the problem of Cuddesdon. The first aspect of that problem is the inaccessibility of the place itself. I am informed that on three days of the week it is entirely without a bus service, and that only on Saturdays and

Sundays does any bus leave or return to the village after four o'clock in the afternoon. This means that as a centre for interviews the place is virtually useless.

His solution was to expand his predecessor's practice of interviewing in the diocesan offices in St Aldate's, and he was keen on moving secretarial and office support there as well. He then went on to complain about the house itself: 'Here I will speak quite frankly. Cuddesdon is in many respects a fine building ... But, judged by even the most modest of modern standards, it is a quite unusually inconvenient house.' To bring it up to modern standards, where 22 bedrooms would never be required, would, he felt, be an enormous task. Although a close friend of Eric Graham's, who had preached at his consecration, Kirk left Cuddesdon, moving to Boar's Hill, as plans were then drawn up for alterations to the palace. A former officer of the College lamented Kirk's decision, making an astute observation: 'It is miserably sad about the Palace. I can see K. E. K.'s point, though I should have thought a measure of inaccessibility was an advantage for a bishop, than otherwise, in these days.'[56]

The war then intervened and, according to Kirk's biographer, Eric Kemp, a fellow bishop of a not dissimilar personality, 'the restrictions of the period 1939-45 showed how fortunate it was that circumstances had caused Kirk to make his home on a reasonable bus route and within ten minutes drive of the cathedral and the Diocesan Office'.[57] During the War Cuddesdon Palace provided a home to the Queen Anne's Bounty (which administered part of the historic resources of the Church of England): about thirty people were billeted in Cuddesdon. In addition the College was requisitioned to house about thirty young Irish women working at Cowley. Two buses would leave the village daily taking them to work. There were two shifts daily from 6am to 2pm and 2pm to 10pm. It was claimed that one woman had practised her embroidery inadvertently making a dress made out of the College altar linen. The War also brought a small contingent from the RAF to Cuddesdon who manned a decoy made of oil tanks in Wellbourne Field which would have been set alight had the Cowley works been subject to German bombing.

After the war the Palace became home to nuns from the Society of the Salutation of St Mary the Virgin from 1946-49 (now part of the double community at Burford). For a period in the war, after Graham had moved to Brechin, the village was served by a curate, Kenneth Jenkins, whose low church ways were greeted positively by a number of parishioners. A number were so impressed by having a priest looking after them who was not also involved in looking after the College that they were reluctant for the next principal to be vicar, fearing another austere regime.

NOTES

1   Order in Council 4 Vict cap. 113.
2   The lack of clarity led to many discussions in the PCC as late as the 1970s about the liability for chancel repairs.
3   Stephen Paget and J.M.C. Crum, *Life of Francis Paget*, London: Macmillan, 1912.
4   'History of Cuddesdon' in *Thame Gazette*, 20 Feb 1951.
5   *Record and Memorial*, 1929, p.120.
6   *The Guardian*, 16 November 1923, p. 1055.
7   *Record and Memorial*, 1929, p. 140.
8   College Newsletter, Trinity 1946.
9   ORO DD Par Cuddesdon b. 6. The *VCH* suggests that the Church was supplied with electricity as early as 1895-6, although it has been impossible to verify this (v, p. 105).
10 G. L. Prestige, *Life of Charles Gore*, London: Heinemann, 1935, p. 325.
11 Prestige, *Life of Charles Gore*, p. 326.
12 See Henry Scott Holland, *'The King of Terrors' or 'Death is Nothing at All'*, Mark D. Chapman (ed.), Cuddesdon: All Saints' PCC, 2003.
13 H. S. Holland, 'Ministry of the Church' in *Creed and Character*, London: Longmans, 1887, pp. 137-40.
14 Stephen Paget (ed.), *Henry Scott Holland. Memoir and Letters*, London: John Murray, 1921, p. 291.
15 *Record and Memorial*, 1929, p.151.
16 The first Minutes Book covers 1917 to 1938. Hereafter MB.
17 MB 23 Dec 1919.
18 MB 18 Feb 1918.
19 MB 1 Oct 1918.
20 MB 1 Oct 1918.
21 MB 24 Jan 1919.
22 *Record and Memorial*, 1929, p.118.
23 MB 20 June 1927.
24 MB 16 Jan 1922.
25 MB 5 April 1926.
26 MB 1 July 1924.
27 MB 5 April 1924.
28 MB 26 March 1928.
29 Letter to Arthur Kemball Cook 27 June 1919 in Lord Charnwood (ed.), *Discourses and Letters of Hubert Murray Burge*, London: Chatto and Windus, 1930, p. 283.
30 Harold Anson, *T. B. Strong*, London: SPCK, 1949, p. 72.
31 Senex, *Oxford Times*, 22 Sept 1978, p. 8.
32 See Robert T. Holtby, *Eric Graham*, London: Oxford University Press, 1967, p. 25.
33 See Holtby, *Eric Graham*, p. 42.
34 Holtby, *Eric Graham*, p. 64.
35 Holtby, *Eric Graham*, p. 67.
36 Holtby (*Graham*, p. 84) recorded this as part of his address at Graham's requiem in Cuddesdon. It does not occur in the published version of the address: Oxford: OUP, 1964.
37 MB 5 May 1929.
38 MB 13 Jan 1930.
39 MB 24 July 1930.

40   MB 6 July 1931.

41   MB 20 Feb 1933.

42   MB 24 Feb 1931.

43   Graham wrote an extensive set of notes on the principles of his scheme of re-ordering which are deposited in ORO, MS DD Par Cuddesdon b. 6.

44   Letter to Graham, 6 April 1935.

45   ORO CPR b. 6. Rogers also made plans for a credence cabinet to be placed south of the Lady Chapel altar.

46   MB 13 Jan 1930.

47   W. M. G. Ducat, *The Story of Cuddesdon Parish Church. A Sermon*, Preached in the Parish Church, November 13, 1887 (privately printed), Oxford, 1887, p.3.

48   ORO CPR b. 6.

49   MB 11 November 1937, 10 February 1938.

50   Holtby, *Graham*, p.69. Harry Luckett wrote in a letter to Kenneth Riches after Fred Sellar's death in 1981 that 'Some told me he was the most clever man at the College'.

51   Plans were recently discovered when clearing out the former College workshops and have been deposited in the College archives.

52   ORO CPR b. 6.

53   Holtby, *Graham*, p.69.

54   MB 11 November 1937.

55   As a sign of his affection for the College, Lang bequeathed an Elizabethan chalice and cover to the College which had been in daily use in his chapel at Lambeth (College Newsletter, Trinity 1946).

56   Holtby, *Graham*, p.27.

57   Eric Kemp, *Kenneth Kirk, Bishop of Oxford, 1937-54*, London: Hodder, 1959, pp. 81-2.

Chapter Ten

From the Second World War to Robert Runcie[1]

Kenneth Riches

Kenneth Riches, who had been working in the Diocese of St Edmundsbury and Ipswich as director of service ordinands, followed Eric Graham as vicar and principal on 3 Feb 1945. A man possessed of great pastoral gifts, he succeeded in rebuilding relations between village and college after the War, partly through his ability to organise a successful fruit and vegetable show which eventually transformed itself into a fete which was held on August Bank Holiday Monday in the palace garden. He also re-introduced bell-ringing, and started a sports club along with a youth club. A member of staff, Ted Shields, organised a successful gymkhana for a number of years, and his wife ran a women's fellowship. The College field was opened up to the village as a cricket ground, and relations greatly improved. During his time in Suffolk Riches had developed a keen interest in gardening and he greatly improved the College gardens, which at the time were maintained by three gardeners. One of his first acts was to remove the hedges around the vicarage, giving a greater sense of unity between principal, college and village.

Riches also re-established the College on a secure footing, modernising its regime and making a few concessions to the increasing number of married students. Various changes were also made to the Church: shortly after his arrival, new and very solid oak communion rails were installed in the sanctuary in 1946 in memory of Bishop Stubbs to the design of H. S. Rogers. The Church was also redecorated under the leadership of the curate, Tony Davies, who wrote his history of the church during this time. The roof of the church was repaired at a cost of over £1500 in 1949. In the same year Riches also sought to clarify ownership of the Reading Room which had gradually mutated into a village hall. Although it had been paid for by the bishop it was not an ecclesiastical building but was held in a trust administered by the Oxford Diocesan Board of Finance. A further complication was that

10.1. Kenneth Riches as Bishop of Lincoln by Penelope Fleming (RCC)

Magdalen College had acquired the freehold from the Earl of Macclesfield when it purchased the estate in 1899. In 1949 there was an agreement to hand over the lease to a 'representative committee of the parish of Cuddesdon' at an annual payment of 2s 4d. to Magdalen College (a sum which was fixed on 30 January 1952), a pittance that was discontinued in the 1970s when the freehold was transferred to the trustees.

On the liturgical front, Riches introduced the 9.30am Parish Communion from 27 May 1945 soon after his installation, a move some in the village found difficult to accept. At first there was an average of only about ten communicants, most people still preferring to communicate at one of the early services. Resistance evidently declined during Riches' incumbency, however, and by 1952 there were about seventy communicants on average (mostly, presumably, students, who would have had little choice). Riches also introduced a Midnight Eucharist at Christmas 1945, a tradition which has continued to the present day. Many famous names visited the parish: 1950 was an especially good year with Michael Ramsey preaching, and Harry Williams leading the Good Friday three-hour devotion. An unusual event of these years was the celebration of an Orthodox liturgy on 8 August 1946 by Hieromonakh Alexis van der Mensbruggke together with a Russian Choir from Paris.

Edward Knapp-Fisher

Edward Knapp-Fisher, who was chaplain at St John's College, Cambridge, having previously been chaplain to Cuddesdon College from 1946-49, succeeded Riches who had been appointed suffragan Bishop of Dorchester and

Archdeacon of Oxford. Knapp-Fisher was inducted on 5 August 1952. He was an altogether different personality from his predecessor. He was something of an ascetic bachelor who lived with his mother, and in some ways he sought to unmodernize the College after Riches' period in charge. His relatively severe regime and spirituality tested the vocations of many students to the limit and there was at times a high drop-out rate. He would often take the students on very long walks. Nevertheless he retained the produce show and proved very popular in the village. At one point he was engaged to a local woman, although this was soon broken off.

10.2. Edward Knapp-Fisher as vicar (RCC)

Many were surprised when it was announced that Knapp-Fisher, while Bishop of Pretoria, was to be married to Joan Bradley, who had been an undergraduate in Oxford and used to visit the village in the 1950s. They married on 17 June 1965, shortly after Knapp-Fisher had published a book *Belief and Prayer*[2] which he dedicated to the parish and college of Cuddesdon.

Shortly after Knapp-Fisher came as vicar and principal the Queen's coronation was marked by the repair of the weathercock by Arthur Smith. A few years later the church underwent some modernisation: a new mains electricity supply was installed as were eight convector heaters in 1955. Heating has proved a perennial problem for the church: earlier in the century, Eric Graham had noted at his first PCC meeting that it had to be addressed as a matter of urgency. However few systems, including 'Mr Clary's pipeless heating' and the convector heaters proved a match for the Cuddesdon chill.[3] The chancel roof was also retiled in Knapp-Fisher's time. It is reported that he was a practical man who enjoyed tractor driving and lawn mowing; he was also renowned as a devilish tennis player.

In 1954 the College celebrated its centenary with a huge rally of former members. The main festival eucharist celebrated by the Archbishop of York on 22 June had 384 communicants. A recording made of the festival service which took place later in the day reflects something of the dying days of Prayer Book worship, with a dirge-like *Te Deum* and public-school style rendition of *Praise My Soul, The King of Heaven*. And it should also be said that the Archbishop of Canterbury's (Geoffrey Fisher) sermon represents one of the low points of Anglican preaching. In 1956 Kenneth Riches returned to preach as Bishop of Lincoln.

During this time there were once again some questions about the future of Cuddesdon Palace which had not been re-occupied after the sisters had moved out in 1949, and which was gradually falling into disrepair. In 1951 Dr Hassall reported that 'The old drive between the elms is choked and the palace stands empty though little changed. Occasionally it is still used for fetes and other local functions.'[4] It was vested with the Church Commissioners on 1 Oct 1954. On 25 January 1955 Harry Carpenter was consecrated bishop of Oxford and shortly afterwards it was decided that he would re-occupy the Palace. To celebrate this return of the Bishop of Oxford to Cuddesdon a lengthy article on Cuddesdon in the *Oxford Mail*[5] interviewed many local residents about their experience of living in the village. Arthur Smith, Parish Clerk and Bullingdon Rural District Council Representative, noted that the village was 'looking forward very much to the new bishop taking up residence in the Palace again because we have no lord of the manor and a village needs a leader.' Other interviews give a vivid picture of life in the village. There was a flourishing football and cricket club as well as a team of bellringers, six of whom were 'ladies'. There were, however, some drawbacks to life in Cuddesdon: although it was relatively close to Oxford, it was badly served by public transport with only three buses a day, and it had yet to be put on mains drainage.

Before the bishop could take up residence in the Palace, however, it was very badly damaged by fire on 11 February 1958, probably through arson, although no cause was ever found; only the Chapel was left intact. The fire was first noticed by a student, Timothy Bravington, soon after 10pm. One of the local residents, Mrs Mary Palmer, of Dove House, also phoned the fire brigade. Although there was scarcely anything of value left inside the Palace, some interesting items did find their way into the hands of local residents after the decision was taken to demolish the ruins. Between thirty and forty firefighters attended from across the area and it was reported that they used water from the College swimming pool.[6] As he noted in his Lent Letter to the former members of the College in 1958, Knapp-Fisher was surprised to hear

Top 10.3. The Palace on Fire (RCC)
Bottom 10.4. The Palace after the Fire (COS)

that the College had a swimming pool: the 'pool' was in fact a stagnant water tank constructed during the war for emergencies. Later in the year a decision was taken by the Commissioners to demolish the ruins of the building.[7] The future of the bishop's connection with Cuddesdon looked precarious.

In January 1959 a Church magazine was started which has survived in various guises down to the present day. At first it had a circulation of about 150 and included a copy of a national church newsletter produced by Mowbray's called *The Sign*.[8] At this period the village was a very active community, with an annual pantomime, a cricket and sports club, as well as a scout group and youth club, both of which were organised by the church and college. A successful fete was held annually on August Bank Holiday Monday, then at the beginning of August, which always raised over £200, and there was also an annual gift day, which made on average slightly short of £100. There were many special services through the church year, including several festal evensongs and a Rogationtide procession. The main church service continued to be the parish communion at 9.30 which was preceded by a sparsely attended matins at 8.45. The quality of worship was high and the Home Service came regularly to Cuddesdon, broadcasting services on at least four occasions during the 1950s and 60s.

The bulk of pastoral work was undertaken by the curate of the village, who was also a part-time member of the College staff. Some notable figures occupied this position. In 1955, for instance, John Austin Baker served as curate and tutor in Old Testament at the College following his ordination at Trinity 1955. Baker eventually went on to become Bishop of Salisbury and one of the most influential churchmen of his generation. At Cuddesdon he was well-known for his prowess at amateur dramatics. In an interview in the *Oxford Mail* he spoke of the 'very close union between the college, the church and the village. We have wonderful services which the students attend as ordinary parishioners. There is a very cordial relationship between the villagers and the students and we find that the village helps the church and the church helps the village.'[9] In 1959 Baker was followed by John Harry Gerald Ruston, who became Bishop of St Helena. Ruston was another ascetic character who used to cultivate an allotment, distributing its produce to the needy of the parish. The clergy letters in the early magazines provide an interesting local gloss on world events. For instance, in a rather touching (if unrealistic) letter written during the rail dispute of August 1959, Knapp-Fisher thought the 'only solution then in any and every dispute, the only hope for mankind, is the eradication of selfishness'.[10]

Not long afterwards, however, the vicar was to experience a rather more serious political crisis at first-hand: he left the parish for a period at the end of 1959 to take an ordination retreat in Grahamstown in South Africa. He wrote back in January 1960: 'I am most impressed by the completely natural way in which we are all living together with the Bishop in his house. The Africans are as much at their ease as we are, and nobody minds or takes any notice if they do anything slightly unusual.'[11] Such an inclusive attitude was frowned upon in South Africa at the time, and after the Sharpeville Massacre a few weeks later, Knapp-Fisher became increasingly aware of the seriousness of the situation. He wrote in April 1960: 'If we rightly condemn the policies of the South African Government as a principal cause of the present catastrophe, we cannot in justice acquit ourselves of any responsibility for it.'[12]

Shortly afterwards in May 1960 the vicar wrote again to his parishioners: 'Owing to the situation in South Africa, I have been compelled to accede to the urgent request of the Archbishop of Cape Town and the other South African bishops that I should go out to Pretoria with as little delay as possible.' He left on 7 June to be consecrated bishop of Pretoria on 19 June, and was enthroned in the cathedral on 23 June. The same position had been held earlier in the century by Michael Furse (1870-1955), the son of a former Principal, who went on to become bishop of St Albans and whose ashes had been interred in the churchyard in 1955. Furse is commemorated by a large stone tablet in the north aisle erected in 1957. In his farewell letter Knapp-Fisher looked back affectionately on his time in Cuddesdon as the 'happiest period' of his life.[13] Shortly before Knapp-Fisher's departure the 8am communion moved to 7.45 in March 1960, presumably to allow more space for matins.

Robert Runcie[14]

Knapp-Fisher was succeeded by Robert Runcie, at the time Dean of Trinity Hall, Cambridge, whose name had been suggested as principal by Owen Chadwick, historian of the College and Runcie's predecessor at Trinity Hall.[15] Even before his induction on 16 September 1960, his family were already settling into parish life, his wife opening the fete on 7 August and the vicar-designate holding a bingo competition at the vicarage afterwards. Runcie's time in Cuddesdon proved a happy and fruitful time for both village and college. His wit, tact, charm and diplomacy won him many friends and admirers. In the first of his vicar's letters he set an agenda for his future ministry, which was more than amply fulfilled: 'I do *not* visualise my job *simply* as getting folk into Church. I want you to feel that you have a friend in your Vicar who cares for this village and cares for you.'[16]

Throughout his time as vicar he made efforts to get to know all the parish-

10.5. Robert Runcie as Vicar of Cuddesdon. Drawing by Penelope Fleming (RCC)

ioners and to involve himself in as full a way as possible in village activities. He wrote again in January 1961 praying that 'we may all involve ourselves in the common task so that Church and Community, young and old, farm worker and factory worker may come together in a healthy and lively Cuddesdon'. The tone of his letters continued to be optimistic and inclusive, but on occasion they could be decidedly challenging. In June 1962, for instance, he wrote: 'If the Church looks dead, it may be because we are dead. … If the Church isn't a real family of brothers and sisters in Christ, whose fault is that but ours?' Given Runcie's later reputation it is interesting to note that his letters never mentioned politics, although in 1964 he did suggest that Christians ought to vote, but without mentioning for which party.

Runcie's concern about the inclusiveness of the village was also reflected in an increasing anxiety about its social mix. He felt it lacked a significant professional middle class. His solution was to build a new housing estate on land from the Bishop's wood. 'What we need,' he told the Church Commissioners in his inimitable way, 'is to create a little Guildford in this wood. It mustn't be too large; it mustn't swamp the village. But we need a middle-class, and if you can build some middle-class housing, it will bring some sort of leadership into the village.'[17] Planning permission was granted in September 1963, and the first three houses occupied by October 1966. With his usual wit, he reported in the College Lent Letter for 1966 that '"Held inert twixt fascination of all opposites" we remain on the edge of the London commuter belt, now officially a hundred miles across, and in the other direction Cowley impinges on us as a bright light in the evening sky and a steady throb of production lines after the compline silence. Only the Church Commissioners are busy building in our island calm, and they seem to be rapidly producing Kensington in the Bishop's Wood ("accommodation for three cars") and Chelsea in his vegetable garden (accommodation for two cars?); but we are promised decent screening.'[18] The changed housing pattern which resulted has undoubtedly had a powerful effect on the nature of village and church life. There have been further small developments since with many of the incomers contributing much to the life of the village.

Shortly before Runcie's appointment a decision had been made by the Church Commissioners and the diocese to build a new and rather more modest house for the bishop, which to contemporary tastes is a remarkably ugly, utilitarian and unimpressive building, but which is typical of an undistinguished period in architecture (and almost identical to the Bishop of Manchester's house). It was gratefully occupied by Harry Carpenter and his family and officially opened on 7 November 1962. The house may have been more modest than its predecessors, but still had ten bedrooms, and five reception rooms. The *Oxford Mail* briefly reported on the opening of the new house, noting the bishop as saying: 'For the first time I have somewhere to work'[19] although there is little sign of his indolence beforehand. This move back to Cuddesdon was greeted with great pleasure by Eric Graham, then Bishop of Brechin. In the long term, however, the house did not prove a success.

Runcie also proved an admirable ecclesiastical diplomat in Cuddesdon, a skill which he needed to exercise again later in his career: much of this involved the introduction of liturgical change, which in the 1960s was rapid. Runcie often spoke of the need to overcome the divide between clergy and laity,[20] and was keen on introducing new and more inclusive styles of worship. After a brief period of discussion on Monday evenings, the New English Bible was being used for the second lesson at Evensong, and, shortly afterwards, by June 1961, for the parish communion itself. In 1962 he introduced an evening service on Maundy Thursday, together with the blessing of the water and renewal of baptismal vows on Holy Saturday evening. Changing patterns of rural life meant that there was no longer any demand for the monthly 7am celebration (aimed at farmers) which was finally abolished in May 1965. Changes continued through the decade and were usually initiated by the vicar through careful preparation of the over large PCC (which had more than 20 members) and the parish.

A fascinating example of an attempt to be relevant was a broadcast parish communion of 29 August 1965 where a 'popular' music mass setting ('The St Andrew Mass' by Malcolm Williamson) accompanied the traditional Prayer

Book service. All the hymns were music hall type settings of traditional hymns by Gordon Hartless, Lancelot Hankey and Michael Brierley. The current bishop of Ely, Anthony Russell, then a student, featured (somewhat implausibly) on the drums, and the choir was directed by Nigel McCulloch, now bishop of Manchester. After the service Runcie remarked that he had received over 100 letters, most of which were positive, although one thought the music hideous, and another asked why the vicar had forgotten to mention 'where coshes, studded belts, etc. should be placed on entering the church, and if purple hearts were on sale in the vestry'.[21] This is probably rather a harsh assessment: a recording of the service now sounds embarrassing, but hardly threatening. Runcie's sermon says much about his obvious dislike of the music (which was indeed fairly hideous), but also his belief that one needed to make sacrifices of taste for the sake of the Gospel.

Shortly after this service, changes were made to the parish communion service in response to the liturgical movement then sweeping through Western Christendom initiated by the Second Vatican Council. Runcie wrote a long editorial in the Parish Magazine in November 1965 calling for greater simplicity and clarity, as well as greater congregational participation. He proposed that the first half of the parish communion service would be led from a lectern in the body of the church, the priest not going to the altar until the offertory. He was also to face the people, the rationale being that 'By seeing the actions which he does in their name, the people will be more able to participate in them. They will feel less like spectators, and more like a family round a table.' The eminently clubbable Runcie thus succeeded in informalising the worship, without apparently encountering much opposition.

Perhaps to appease the traditionalists, it was decided not long afterwards to use the east-facing high altar for the 7.45 celebration. In 1967 the Revised Standard Version began to be used for the readings, and in July of that year a 'liturgy committee' was established on the PCC to implement the new services (Series II) which had at long last been produced by the Church of England as a supplement to the Prayer Book. Runcie's aim was to create what he called 'local experts' so that the PCC and congregation might be 'guided by knowledge, and not just by prejudice or fancy, when they come to decide on whether they like the new services or not'.[22] This clever means for deflecting any potential opposition by creating liturgical 'expertise' meant that the new services were introduced 'experimentally' with the minimum of fuss in September, and then permanently from Advent Sunday 1967, with a course of sermons explaining what was going on. Again Runcie's principles of inclusion were to the fore: 'The old service depended almost entirely on the Parson. The new service depends on everyone taking their part in the team.'[23] The 7.45 service, which returned to 8am in 1969, remained a Prayer Book celebration.

In 1962 Runcie's curate, Ruston followed his former vicar to South Africa, remaining there until 1991, having become suffragan bishop in the diocese of Pretoria in 1983. From 1991 to 1999 he was Bishop of St Helena. He was replaced as curate by the young Peter Cornwell, the first of a series of distinguished curates appointed by Runcie. Cornwell was soon promoted to Vice-Principal, remaining at the College until 1966, and going on to be vicar of the University Church in Oxford, before converting to the Roman Catholic Church. He was succeeded as curate in 1963 by Mark Santer, who had been ordained to the college staff and curacy in 1963 and who ended his career as bishop of Birmingham. As well as carrying out most of the pastoral responsibilities, the lot of the curate was to help run the youth club, which was done with more or less success, some future bishops proving more adept in disciplining the youth of Cuddesdon than others. Activities at the time included folk dancing for which few had been prepared in their theological education. Other village groups proved less successful: the Scout Troop, which had been run by students, eventually folded in June 1964.

The village and church were also fortunate in having Mark Carpenter-Garnier, who had been Bishop of Colombo, living in the Old Vicarage during this time: he was a very regular and reliable celebrant at the early communions in the church, and nothing, not even a disastrous snowfall, prevented his getting to church. When he left the village Runcie wrote of his 'punctilious reliability'. He was also a benefactor of the church, donating the fine festal vestments in February 1967. He was less enthusiastic about the Church fete and strongly disapproved of raffles, always taking his holiday a week on either side of August Bank Holiday. After his wife died at the end of 1967, he remained living in Cuddesdon for a short time, leaving the village in October 1968. His death on 11 October 1969 was announced shortly before Runcie's departure and described as the 'end of an era'.[24] Carpenter-Garnier left £500 to the church[25] and a memorial plaque was dedicated on All Saints' Day 1973 in memory of the bishop and his wife at a cost of £46.65. Another bishop was to follow him into the Old Vicarage: after a period of rumour, it was announced in October 1969 that Michael Ramsey, archbishop of Canterbury and a former student, would be coming to live there on his retirement.

The Church building underwent some major maintenance during Runcie's time as vicar, beginning with an extensive set of repairs to the tower in 1962 which involved rebuilding the parapet. Shortly afterwards, the old Hammond Organ reached the end of its life, and a new instrument was installed in November 1962, initially with a rotating speaker, more often used by jazz

10.6. Church from North Side after removal of pinnacles (MC)

organists. Not surprisingly, the vicar's letter of December began, 'Don't shoot the organist!' The problems were finally rectified by July 1963. However, despite great hope at the installation, it did not prove a fine instrument and was replaced by a pipe organ twenty years later. By 1965 both porches were in need of restoration, and other substantial work was carried out to the north aisle and the chancel glass. In 1966 the interior was redecorated along the same lines as before, which, Runcie noted, 'should avoid the controversy which frequently attends the redecoration of the church'. At the same time a cupboard was created from the rear pews at the back of the south aisle for flower vases and a large box was built around the electrical apparatus in the south transept. On 13 July 1967, during a dramatic thunderstorm, one of the pinnacles on the tower collapsed into the North Transept, causing a large amount of damage: repairs were urgently required, and it was decided that since the pinnacles did little to beautify the church, they would not be replaced. This would have pleased Alfred Pott who had sought to remove them over a century before. The re-roofing of the transept was completed in July 1968. Perhaps not surprisingly the Church fell into debt which led to a scheme for covenanting and the begin-ning of an envelope scheme for giving, which continues to the present day.

Runcie's series of able curates and colleagues continued, with many going on to hold high office in the Church. Shortly before Knapp-Fisher's surprise engagement was announced, Runcie had appointed a new chaplain, Jeremy Saville, in April 1965, which reflects something of the changed conditions under Runcie's regime: 'He is unmarried and lives in College, which – as you may murmur – is how they all start'. When Mark Santer left to go to Clare College, Cambridge as dean, he was succeeded by Michael Scott-Joynt who was ordained to the curacy as deacon in 1967, and has gone on to become Bishop of Winchester. All the College staff ministered in the church and were regular preachers at the parish communion, and, given the subsequent career of many of the clergy, the standard of preaching was presumably high, with several series of sermons on the great themes of the day, including in Lent 1967 a set on 'great contemporary leaders of the church' from Pope John to the East Harlem Parish.

As vicar Runcie also displayed his powers of diplomacy outside the church especially in his relationships with the Parish Council where a strong influence was the village Garage proprietor, Arthur Smith. When Colonel Bowes of Chippinghurst Manor had to stand down through illness, Runcie went on to succeed him as chairman of the Council in 1967. His negotiations with the various interest groups in the village were sensitive and he managed to improve the strained relations between college and village. On the whole (although not always) he was successful in handling conflict. At one point he even became involved in the village hall committee. Runcie was probably at his happiest addressing the small village congregation during the College vacations, which was often joined by a visiting ecclesiastical dignitary staying at the new Bishop's House.

As principal he slowly liberalised the College regime, eventually allowing women (including wives) into the College building as occasional guests. He also improved links with the University and steered a steady path through the heated theological debates of the 1960s. Indeed Cuddesdon College began to be seen as the intellectual power house among the theological colleges during this time: for instance a parish communion was broadcast nationally on the theme of 'The Temptations of the Affluent Society' in 1961. Various initiatives and study groups were organised through the decade, with the Lent Course for 1964 appropriately entitled, 'Christianity in the 1960s'.

By the late 1960s Runcie was beginning to look to move on partly no doubt because the work of college principal was proving increasingly difficult to combine with that of vicar: the professionalisation of clergy training was becoming ever more stressful for a college principal, without the added burden of pastoral care for a small village with high expectations of its clergy. Furthermore, a report had been commissioned by the church authorities to discuss the future of theological education: there had been a sharp decline in the number of ordinands which meant that some rationalisation would soon be needed.

Runcie wrote a letter to his erstwhile curate, Ruston on 4 November 1969, with which he enclosed a copy of the parish magazine:

> Now our roots are very deep. I feel that the work has built up so much over the last year or so that in some ways another man should write the next chapter, but on personal grounds Lindy is very happy here and she hates the thought of uprooting after having made this house so lovely and got the children so well settled at school.[26]

He declined the offer of the deanery of Guildford, but accepted the Bishopric of St Albans, announcing his departure in November 1969. He always regretted not having more time for the parish, because running the college had always had first claim on his time. Nevertheless he wrote touchingly: 'So far as I am personally concerned I would have found myself much less happily engaged with my work if it had not given me the opportunity for involvement in the life and interest of the local community.'

As a parting shot, Runcie announced that the pastoral arrangement for the village would change: both vicar and curate were finding it increasingly difficult to meet pastoral needs, which meant that Michael Scott-Joynt would also be giving up his work in the parish though remaining on the college staff. The Bishop of Oxford consequently announced that although the principal would remain as vicar, he should not normally be expected to carry out the day-to-day pastoral work, which was to devolve more heavily on the curate. It was therefore announced that John Selby, who had been working since 1964 as chaplain to Mark Carpenter-Garnier and as bursar in the College, and who had been ordained late in life after a career in the Nigerian Civil Service, would take over as curate, giving up his college post. He began his dedicated service as curate, of decided Anglo-Catholic leanings, in March 1970. In the early 1970s, Fr Selby, as he was styled by many, was organising trips to the National Pilgrimage at Walsingham on Spring Bank Holiday.

In his final letter of February 1970, Runcie noted the changes in village life over the ten years he had served as incumbent. Sport, drama, scouts, and youth clubs had all declined, but nevertheless, he noted, 'Cuddesdon remains recognisably a village and even as the population changes, fresh opportunities open up and new patterns of life emerge, it is crucial that we don't lose touch with each other.' He finished his ministry as he started: 'The Church is not just a bit of village life, and yet there is a sense in which it fails to be true to itself if it is not always related to the community in which it is set'. Indeed, he went on, the role of Christians in the modern world, was to be 'community builders'.

Unlike many of his predecessors Runcie enjoyed being vicar of a country parish, and the memory of Cuddesdon remained a constant source of inspiration throughout his often troubled primacy in the 1980s. He wrote on leaving the parish: 'The worship and atmosphere of Cuddesdon Church will remain an inspiration to me all my life. The past few years have shown there is plenty of life within and emanating from its walls. The new services have been welcomed and there are opportunities for those who prefer the old ways.' Finally, he told his parishioners for the last time, '[my] feelings are of overwhelming gratitude for your friendship and patience. ... I will treasure the privilege of being welcomed in your homes at the grave and the gay, the significant and the ordinary moments of human life'. The feeling was usually mutual: Runcie is affectionately remembered by many in the village. One of his last public acts before his death in the summer of 2000 was to open the Church fete where his charm and wit, along with his extraordinary capacity to remember people's names and to treat them as if they mattered, were brilliantly displayed for a final time. It came as no surprise that when he was elevated to the peerage on his retirement as archbishop, he chose the title, 'Runcie of Cuddesdon'.

NOTES

1   Unless otherwise stated, information from this period is taken from the Parish records in the ORO, the parish newsletters and the church archive as well as interviews with residents and former residents of the village and college. The individual items in the miscellaneous papers are not catalogued in the ORO.

2   London: Darton, Longman and Todd, 1964.

3   MB 5 February 1929.

4   'The History of Cuddesdon' in *Thame Gazette*, 20 Feb 1951.

5   26 January 1956, p. 6.

6   *Oxford Times*, 14 Feb 1958. There had been an earlier fire in 1956.

7   *Reading Mercury*, 2 Aug 1958, p. 9.

8   ORO DD Par Cuddesdon b. 6 (h). The circulation in 1960 was 57 to the College and 94 to the village.

9   *Oxford Mail*, 20 January 1956, p. 6.

10   *All Saints' News* (hereafter *ASN*), August 1959.

11   *ASN* Jan 1960

12   *ASN* April 1960.

13   *ASN* June 1960.

14   On Robert Runcie's time at Cuddesdon, see Margaret Duggan, *Runcie. The Making of an Archbishop*, London: Hodder and Stoughton, 1983, chapters 9 and 10; and Humphrey Carpenter, *Robert Runcie. The Reluctant Archbishop*, London: Hodder and Stoughton, 1996, chapter 9.

15   For the circumstances of Runcie's appointment, see Mark D. Chapman, 'The Triumph of Wit: The Runcie Years' in *Ambassadors of Christ*, Aldershot: Ashgate, 2004, ch. 6.

16   *ASN* Oct 1960.

17   Carpenter, *Robert Runcie*, p. 155.
18   Cuddesdon College Lent Letter, 1966 (CCA LL23).
19   *Oxford Mail*, 7 Nov 1962.
20   E.g. vicar's letter, *ASN*, May 1964.
21   *ASN*, Oct 1965.
22   *ASN* July 1967.
23   *ASN* Dec 1967.
24   *ASN* Nov 1969.
25   The PCC Minutes Book exists from the Church Annual General Meeting of 31 March 1970. Hereafter *MB*.
26   ORO DD Par Cuddesdon b. 6 (h). Some in the village found Lindy Runcie's detachment from life in College and Village difficult to understand.

Chapter Eleven

Leslie Houlden to the Present Day

Leslie Houlden and Cuddesdon

Robert Runcie was succeeded by (James) Leslie Houlden, a leading New Testament scholar, who had been Chaplain and Fellow of Trinity College, Oxford. He was presented by the Lord Chancellor and inducted on 17 July 1970. In his first letter he noted the many changes he had detected in the village and college since his own time as a student from 1953-55, observing the 'new houses, the coming of light industry, and the feeling that Oxford is nearer than it was. The presence of a number of married students and their wives means that college and village intertwine in a way they did not, even so short a time ago.' Similarly, it appeared to him that the congregation had grown more diverse. The new vicar expressed his hope that he would soon get to know the many different people who made up the Christian community.[1]

Parish life continued much as before with the occasional heated dispute between residents of the village – the PCC Minutes Book contains occasional references to conflicts over such matters as the use of the churchyard as a short cut from Dove House to the village.[2] Similarly, the purchase of grass seed for the path from the Bishop's house and the purchase and maintenance of motor mowers seem to have provoked an undue amount of discussion.[3] Other things seem to have less problematic: the congregation quickly settled into the new Series II communion service and gradually adopted other changes, including an offertory procession from April 1972. In October 1973 it was announced that the Series III service would be adopted from Advent, after a test run on 14 October. It was initially trialled for a period of five months, and after 'much discussion', its use was extended to Easter subject to review at the AGM.[4] However, the matter does not seem to have been discussed at the AGM and the new service continued until 1980 and the introduction of the *Alternative Service Book*, although there were evidently some dissenting voices

11.1. Leslie Houlden as Vicar of Cuddesdon (RCC)

on the PCC.[5] In June 1975 Fr Selby announced his retirement to Ladder Hill in Wheatley, having shown an 'unobtrusive' but also 'remarkable' service particularly to the young and to the sick.[6] He was replaced on a part-time basis by Brian Smith in July, who was also a tutor at the college, the curacy once again becoming a part-time post. He has since become Bishop of Edinburgh. One of the new curate's first suggestions was for coffee after the service once a month, a practice that seems to have caused remarkably little discussion.[7]

As always, the fabric of the church was a cause of concern. In 1971 extensive work was completed on the gutters, and by April 1973, the medieval Parish Cross, which had moved to its position by the west porch of the church in Victorian times, had deteriorated to such a degree that it had to be dismantled.[8] Its base still stands. Major repairs were made to the South Transept roof in the summer of 1977 and at the same time the west window was releaded. The fete, the major fund-raising event of the church year for such costly undertakings, moved from August Bank Holiday to the beginning of June in 1972, which allowed students to play a full part in running stalls after the abolition of the Summer Vacation Term. As a result the takings increased by twenty percent.

The village School had been proving a cause of concern for some time. As early as 1962 numbers had dropped to a mere sixteen: the school's future was being discussed throughout the 1960s and at the beginning of 1971 a public meeting heard that the school would close in July 1972. By this stage it was only educating children of infant age, with older children being bussed to Garsington. After 1972 all the primary school-age children attended

Garsington School. Mrs Edwards retired in 1972 after twenty-four years as headmistress. Also in 1972 the sports club was wound up through lack of volunteers. Another amenity was also lost at this time: buses had always been rare in the village, but by the mid-1970s, it was announced that the service would be discontinued altogether in September 1977, although a brief reprieve saw two services a week to Oxford on Wednesdays and Saturdays for a while. The final bus ran on 24 February 1980.

By 1973, however, other aspects of village life began to pick up – the parish newsletter was transformed in March 1973 to a village newspaper called Cuddesdon News, and edited by a student named Stephen Platten, who has since become Bishop of Wakefield. This paper was soon announcing a revival of the Cuddesdon Amateur Dramatic Society. Bellringing was also re-established with regular practices on Tuesdays, and by 1975 there was a Scottish Country dancing club in the village hall. As announced before his retirement, Michael Ramsey had come to live at the Old Vicarage: one of his first acts on moving to the village in 1974 was to open the new extension to the Village Hall in December of that year.[9] There were also a number of gifted laity involved in the church and village including a retired general secretary of the Church of England Central Advisory Council on Training for the Ministry, W. H. Saumarez-Smith, who succeeded Runcie as chairman of the Parish Council.

Soon after Houlden's appointment, Harry Carpenter resigned as bishop of Oxford, celebrating in Cuddesdon church for the last time on 6 December 1970. He was succeeded by Kenneth Woollcombe who was enthroned on 27 March 1971. He found the Bishop's House, with its substantial gardens, something of a burden, particularly after the tragic death of his wife on 6 August 1976. Shortly beforehand, the village suffered another tragedy when Ian Denby, a vet, took his own life. Not long after Gwenda Woollcombe's death the Bishop moved out of the house at Easter 1978 and resigned soon afterwards. Patrick Rodger, Woollcombe's successor, decided against living in Cuddesdon. The *Oxford Times* reported that Woollcombe had 'announced that he was seeking a new house and this has been reiterated by his successor who wishes to live in the country but somewhere nearer the heart of things'.[10] The house eventually chosen was in Linton Road, North Oxford, hardly in the country, but possibly more in the heart of things than Cuddesdon. The Bishop's House in Cuddesdon was consequently put on the market and auctioned by E. J. Brooks on 26 September 1978.[11] The four-hundred year-old connection between bishop and village was thus ended. Initially the house became a retreat house belonging to Toc H, which over the years contributed a great deal to the life of the village. A weekly communion service was held on Wednesdays in the restored chapel from 1983. However, after a financial crisis in Toc H, the house was sold in 1996 as a private house, initially to a minor television celebrity.

The College was undergoing major re-organisation during this period. After some sensitive negotiations Cuddesdon College amalgamated in 1975 with Ripon Hall, a Modernist foundation which had been situated on Boar's Hill on the other side of Oxford. Houlden's energies were concentrated on the delicate issue of the amalgamation. Although it had initially been agreed that both principals would resign, Houlden stayed on as interim Principal for a further two years, announcing his intention to resign in March 1977. He took immediate 'extended leave' from the parish, finally departing on 30 September. The first years of the new College did not prove easy either for the students or the two principals. In addition, three other members of the College staff also resigned in 1977.

Michael Ramsey did not stay long in Cuddesdon. Initially he enjoyed renewing the connection with the college (where he had been a student in 1928) and the parish church, where he preached regularly, but he felt increasingly isolated and distant from the academic world. This was compounded when his trusty housekeeper and chauffeuse had to give up. An immensely shy man, he did not adjust to life in a small village. He also found some of the problems associated with the union of the two colleges difficult to bear and he and his wife left Cuddesdon for Durham in May 1977.[12]

Leslie Houlden took up a senior lectureship at King's College, London, becoming professor in 1987. One of his last acts as vicar was to invite Christopher Evans, who was retiring as Professor of New Testament at King's, to live in one of the Church Commissioners' bungalows that had been part of the Bishop's House property. Since then Professor Evans has been regularly taking the early Sunday communion service. Mr Rhodes, who had been churchwarden, gave the farewell address for Houlden at the end of August: 'Over the years I think we have all been impressed by his wise judgements, and by the ease with which he seems to take all difficulties in his stride. We shall miss him very much – but we shall remember gratefully the calm, unhurried and friendly way in which he has at all times dealt with our parish problems.'[13] However, there was evidently some conflict both in the village and college at the time: Brian Smith, the curate, wrote that 'We must let this place be a place where love may grow between us all, where bitterness and resentment are allowed to die, where mutual understanding and compassion may flourish, so that our life here together may conform to the pattern which we know is God's will for us all.'

Another retirement was announced in 1977, this time of Fred Sellar, a farmer from Denton, who had served as churchwarden since the War, to be replaced initially by his son, Cyril. Fred, a stalwart of the 8am congregation, died in 1981, Robert Runcie sending a personal letter of condolence to his family.[14] 1977 also saw festivities for the Silver Jubilee of the Queen. These were rather more modest than those of ninety years earlier, with a parade from Parkside to the Recreation Ground followed by dancing to Smokey Joe's Country and Western Band. Unlike for Queen Victoria there does not appear to have been any free beer.[15]

David Wilcox

David Wilcox followed Leslie Houlden as Principal in 1977 and was initially licensed as priest-in-charge on 25 October, primarily because the College was considering a move to Manchester. The PCC was anxious about losing its vicar and made representations to the Bishop after a special meeting on 15 March 1977 hoping that the past arrangement with the Principal as vicar would continue (and in the process also asking for a married man).[16] With some of the proceeds from the sale of Ripon Hall, the College had bought the freehold of the Old Vicarage, which now served as the principal's (and vicar's) residence. It was probably unique to Cuddesdon that for about twenty years the vicar lived in the Old Vicarage, even though there had been no 'old vicar' to house after 1637. The vicarage itself, now referred to as College House, was converted to offices, flats and teaching rooms. The Governors eventually decided not to move to Manchester and in June 1978 the news was announced to the parish.

In June 1979 Brian Smith resigned as curate to take up the post of director of training in Wakefield diocese and priest in charge of Cragg Vale near Halifax. He was replaced by Martin Wharton, Director of Pastoral Studies at the College, and now Bishop of Newcastle, who had been on the College staff from 1977.[17] At this time, plans were made to celebrate the eight-hundredth anniversary of the building of the Church in 1180, with a number of activities, culminating in a service on the patronal festival with Robert Runcie, who had recently been appointed archbishop of Canterbury, as preacher. He came on All Saints' Day (1 November) to preach at choral evensong, which was relayed on Radio Oxford. This was followed by a reception at the village hall with a 'stand up buffet of substantial proportions'. Mrs Wyn Sellar baked a cake for the occasion. The following day Runcie presided at the patronal festival after which a cherry tree was planted near the west porch of the church.[18]

Other activities included a lecture by Dr Hassall on the early history of the village in March, a festival evensong in June with Kenneth Riches, and in

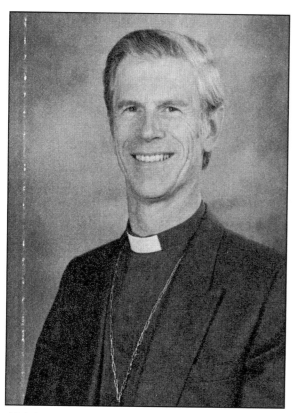

11.2. David Wilcox as Bishop of Dorking (RCC)

October a specially-commissioned play by Maida Stainer entitled 'A Distant View'.[19] According to *Cuddesdon News*, the play was 'brilliantly carried off'. As part of the celebrations new green vestments and an altar frontal were donated to the church, and the college donated a new set of Lenten vestments.[20] A small booklet, with some inaccuracies, was also produced for sale at the back of the church. 1980 also saw the death of Arthur Smith, stalwart of the Parish Council, and proprietor of the garage.[21]

1980 was marked liturgically by the launch of the short-lived *Alternative Service Book*, which was introduced at the beginning of 1981, again with few difficulties. The congregation had been prepared for the new book by Geoffrey Cuming, the eminent liturgist, who was on the staff of the College. After a year's trial several points were discussed and it seems that the peace was shared with a handshake following a decision made at the PCC meeting on 10 November 1982.[22] By 1985 David Wilcox expressed some dissatisfaction with the ASB, particularly its non-inclusive language.[23] A Liturgy Committee was established which led to the purchase of *Hymns Ancient and Modern New Standard* to replace the *English Hymnal* with supplements. The book was eventually bought in 1986.

Early in 1982, David Wilcox produced a discussion paper 'Taking Stock,' which challenged the congregation to greater social involvement and a focus on mission rather than simply 'maintaining the church as an institution',[24] although it is not clear quite what effect this had on the parish. Wilcox was collated as vicar on 22 December 1982 and the College gradually began to settle down in its new guise as Ripon College. A successful Ball was begun in the summer of 1981 which has continued until recently, and in the same year the first women were admitted as students.

Continued improvements were made to the church during this period: the 1960s Hammond Organ was reaching the end of its life, and spare parts were no longer obtainable. After lengthy discussions which began in 1979, a decision was made to replace it with a second-hand pipe organ. By July 1981 the old organ was in such a state of disrepair (it had 'had it', as Mr Saumarez-Smith reported to the PCC) that there was a renewed sense of urgency.[25] After consultation with Edward Higginbottom, director of music at New College, a decision was made to acquire a Victorian Willis organ (after some competition with Norwich School) which had been in temporary use at Christ Church Cathedral during the construction of its new organ and which had originally been built for the chapel of St Margaret's Convent, East Grinstead.[26] Christ Church had agreed with Norwich School that the figure for dismantling and removal should be £5,000 but a further concession was made to the church which allowed them to spread the cost over three years.[27] Bishop and Sons organ builders of Ipswich estimated the cost for rebuilding the organ at £2048 plus board and lodging for the labourers.[28] To raise money a special organ appeal was launched. Like the earlier pipe organ the new organ was positioned in the north transept, more on aesthetic than on acoustic grounds. The floor of the transept had to be raised by six inches and some memorial tablets unfortunately had to be covered up. The new instrument was dedicated on Easter Eve, 10 April 1982.

The decision to buy a new organ was partly the result of a joint working party which had been formed between members of the PCC and the College. Various other suggestions coming from this group were put into effect in the next few years.[29] Shortly after the installation of the organ, the church was rewired and relit by a dedicated team of volunteers. The new lighting was first used on Maundy Thursday, 4 April 1985 with an official switching-on ceremony on 9 June and a blessing on 3 November.[30] A new heating system was installed in October 1986 at the cost of about £1500. This was modelled on a system in use at Great Tew, which was 'supposedly quite economical to run'.[31] Its economy derives primarily from its ineffectiveness and Cuddesdon remains what must be one of the coldest churches in England (presumably along with Great Tew).

In September 1983 Martin Wharton left to take up a post as Director of Training in Bradford and was succeeded by Alistair Redfern, who is now Bishop of Grantham. Redfern quickly established himself as an energetic curate devoting much time to work with families. This affected the liturgical life of the church: from September 1984 the first Sunday of the month parish communion became a 'family communion'.[32] David Wilcox took his last service on 29 December 1985, becoming Bishop of Dorking the following year. His energy, commitment, and practical help were much appreciated by the PCC, the churchwarden, John Paxton, noting that 'in working parties it was always the vicar on top of the highest ladder'.[33]

John Garton

David Wilcox was succeeded by the energetic ex-guardsman, John Garton, who moved to Cuddesdon from being Team Rector of a deprived part of Coventry. He was inducted on 25 April 1986. In his first letter he outlined his approach to ministry: 'I believe that a life in the service of God has to be rooted in a firm but flexible discipline of prayer and worship enriched by theological reflections'.[34] This passionate asceticism was combined with an ability to raise large amounts of money. Shortly after John Garton's arrival a visiting student from the USA died of an AIDS-related illness, one of the first such deaths in Oxfordshire. This led to some sensitive discussions in the PCC about the sharing of the chalice. Eventually it was decided to introduce the practice of intinction at the 9.30 parish communion 'pending further inquiries'.[35] Despite these enquiries, which showed that there was no risk from sharing the chalice, this practice continued among some members of the congregation for some time. Other (less sensitive) questions resulted from vandalism to the pulpit, candlesticks and crucifix, as well as the central lancet window in the south aisle.[36] A new and striking window of the ascension of Elijah was commissioned from Joseph Nuttgens of High Wycombe. Its bright colours clash with its Victorian neighbours.

In May 1987 it was announced that Alistair Redfern was leaving to become Director of Training in Bristol. This brought to a head the problem of pastoral care of the village since there was no suitable member of staff at the College to replace him, which meant that for a time Garton had to combine being principal with the pastoral care of the village. This put the vicar in an unenviable position. The college had grown in size and the job of the principal had become ever more complex and time-consuming: the increasingly close links with the university, the growing numbers of married students, together with the proliferation of new pastoral and mission courses all added to the administrative burden of the college staff. There was a long discussion in the PCC in 1987 about the future of the pastoral care of the village.

John Garton expressed concern about the impossibility of adequately combining the different roles and of how easy it was for both vicar and curate to feel guilty that they were not devoting sufficient time to either parish or college. With his typical vigour he pressed the case for a woman deacon, and also reported that he had persuaded the diocese to make up half the costs of a stipend (a very generous offer given the size of the village and the numbers of resident clergy). Also mooted for the first time was the possibility of links with other parishes.[37] Later in the year it was suggested that an American, Mrs Pinkerton, who had

11.3. John Garton as Vicar (RCC)

been ordained priest in the USA, might be an appropriate appointment. In the event this proved impossible as the Archbishop of Canterbury was not prepared to license any women ordained abroad, even to work as deacon.

As an interim measure it was arranged for students to help with the visiting, but by August 1988 the curacy was filled by a married job share, which meant that for the first time a woman deacon was ministering in the parish. Jonathan Inkpin and Penny Jones stayed for a couple of years before moving to Gateshead in September 1990. Parish life continued to be full, with meetings about the changing nature of the community and to discuss the Church's response to the *Faith in the City* Report, the vice-principal of the College at the time, Alan Billings, having been one of the commissioners responsible for its production. The Church had also begun to sponsor a CMS missionary, Susan Essam, who was attached to the Bishop of Jos in Nigeria, a link which has continued to the present.

After the arrival of the curates, John Garton was able to devote more time to the development of the college, launching a major fund-raising plan in 1989 to build a large new block of flats for married students which required the ambitious sum of £1,000,000. The appeal was successful and the new building, known as the Runcie Building, was opened by the Duchess of Kent in June 1990. Various repairs were made to the church during John Garton's time – the gable at the west end of the church was repaired in the summer of 1988, and the clock regilded in March 1989. An extensive redecoration of the nave took place in the summer of 1992, with services held temporarily in the College Chapel. Together with the need to replace the coping stones on the roof the costs amounted to £17,000. There were various gifts left to beautify the church, including an embroidered altar cloth donated in memory of the George and Rita Hicks and Michael Sawyer.[38] Christopher Evans donated an altar book for the 8am service. 1990 saw the deaths of several long-standing residents of the village, including Florence Sellar, aged 97, who was Fred's widow. Having lost its bus and school, the village lost yet another vital service during the 1990s: the Post Office ceased trading on 26 September 1991.

In June 1992 Stephanie Bullock, who had trained as a doctor, was ordained deacon to serve as curate in the village and as part-time chaplain in the College. She carried out a diligent regime of visiting and getting to know people, as well as organising successful children's activity days. She was ordained to the priesthood on 17 April 1994, a move which created some dissent within the congregation. Shortly afterwards, at the end of the year, she moved on to work at the Churchill Hospital as a chaplain. The finances of the diocese meant that no more contributions to the costs of a curate would be forthcoming, and the vicar worked with his ordained colleagues looking after the church and parish without the assistance of a curate. The personal strain this double role could place on the vicar was shown in the summer of 1995 after the tragic deaths of a father and young daughter who were members of the congregation.

A combination of retirements and expediency, together with a modicum of strategic planning, led the Archdeacon of Oxford and Bishop of Dorchester to discuss the creation of a new team ministry centred on Wheatley in 1995. In 1996 this materialised with John Fuller, who had served on the staff of the College from 1971 to 1977, being licensed as Team Rector. The PCC held a meeting with the Bishop of Dorchester and voted to join the Team Ministry, although there was little enthusiasm for the scheme. The parish of Cuddesdon was to be 'clustered' with Horspath and Garsington, with the team vicar resident at Garsington. Announcing this to the parish in 1996, John Garton wrote that he would resign as vicar to allow the new Team Vicar of Garsington, Cuddesdon and Horspath to take over. In the event he resigned for other reasons when he was appointed Bishop of Plymouth, and consecrated on 3 July 1996.

The first Team Vicar, Richard Cowles, who had been a student under John Garton and curate in Iffley, was licensed the following September, and in January 1997 the Revd John Clarke, who had been vicar of St Mary's, Battersea, was licensed as Principal. The joint post of vicar and principal, which had lasted nearly 150 years, was thus ended. A Faculty agreement ensures that the College has the right to use the Church for its services in return for an annual charge. Changes on the College staff meant that when the Team Vicar could not take services there was little continuity; in response, the Revd Dr Mark Chapman, Vice-principal of the College, who had previously worked in the Dorchester Team, was licensed as assistant curate in September 1999, thereby renewing the old pattern of a curate who was also a member of the teaching staff.

There the history of Christianity in Cuddesdon ends: what the future holds nobody can tell. All we can say is that the future of the Church in Cuddesdon will undoubtedly be different from its past. There are tentative moves towards closer collaboration with neighbouring parishes. But little can be taken for granted: the deanery of Aston and Cuddesdon is to lose three more stipendiary clergy over the next few years. Changing demography and leisure interests mean that the congregations at both Sunday services have slowly but steadily declined. The College (as was suggested by Eric Graham) now worships separately from the Village except for Harvest Festival at the start of the College year. Its main act of worship is on a Friday evening. And once again the Church of England is reviewing its training programmes for ordinands: the future of the College is far from secure. The beautiful building is expensive to maintain with its exposed position and soft stone and is a severe drain on the finances of an ageing congregation. Nevertheless Cuddesdon's majestic church still stands as a witness to Christianity in this area, just as it has done for over eight hundred years. What is important is that the future generations who live in this parish and who attend the College do not forget their heritage and continue to care for this diocesan and national monument. This little book is written in the hope that something of this heritage might be better known. Far more important, however, is that these future generations do not forget that this and every church should stand as a witness to the Gospel of Jesus Christ – and that is something that needs to be heard afresh in every generation.

NOTES

1   *ASN*, Aug 1970.
2   *MB*, pp. 3, 5, 6.
3   *MB*, pp. 5, 9. Such discussions reveal something of the tensions in village life which were left over from the 1960s.
4   *MB*, pp. 54, 55.
5   *MB*, p. 59.
6   *Cuddesdon News* (hereafter *CN*), June 1975. Fr Selby died in January 1985.
7   *MB* p. 72.
8   *MB* p. 45. The cost for proposed restoration of £465 was considered exorbitant. The 1900 cross head was to be 'retained inside the church for posterity' (p. 49).
9   This replaced an iron hut which had earlier been moved from the Bishop's palace.
10   Senex, *Oxford Times*, 22 Sept 1978, p. 8.
11   The autioneers' catalogue 'The Bishop's House, Cuddesdon' contains a detailed description of the building together with the various covenants attaching to the use of the building: it must not have any name implying a connection with the bishop, and any change of use of the chapel must be approved by the Church Commissioners. The rateable value at the time of purchase was £1,038.
12   Owen Chadwick, *Michael Ramsey. A Life*, Oxford: Oxford University Press, 1991, pp. 382-4
13   *CN* Sept 1977.
14   A copy of a touching letter exists in the Parish Records from Harry Luckett to Kenneth Riches which records something of life in Cuddesdon and Oxford in the early part of the twentieth century. Luckett had worked for the College helping them become more self-sufficient in the production of food. He was responsible for the production of eggs.
15   *MB* p. 81.
16   *MB* pp. 85-6.
17   Martin Wharton served on the Parish Council introducing the carol service and Christmas tree on the new village green.
18   A programme of the activities is included in the parish archives.
19   The excitement of the year was reported in the short-lived *Oxfordshire Life* of February/March 1980, pp. 14-15. The play, which was performed in church and produced by Tony Davis, head of English and Drama at Wheatley Park School, was in part based on the Cuddesdon Mummers play, which was deposited in the public library in 1914. 'A Distant View' has a distinctly mummers feel, with the leading character named Faggoty Man. One of the characters is named Bartholomew Day after the *VCH* error noted above.
20   *MB* p. 143.
21   £250 was donated to the churchyard fund in his memory (*MB* p. 140).
22   *MB* p. 165.
23   *MB* p. 212.
24   *MB* p. 157.
25   *MB* p. 156.
26   An earlier offer of a small 1820 organ from the Bristol area failed to materialise (*MB* p. 110). The specification for the organ is as follows:

Great		Swell	
15th	2ft	Oboe	8ft
Principal	4ft	Gemshorn	4ft
Claribel flute	8ft	Lieblich Gedacht	8ft
Dulciana	8ft	Open Diapason	8ft

Pedal		Couplers
Bourdon	16ft	Swell to great; swell to pedals; great to pedals.

27 The Dean of Christ Church to Wilcox, 16 July 1981, Parish Archives.
28 John Budgen of Bishop's of Ipswich to Keith Randall, 19 July 1981.
29 *MB* p. 120.
30 *MB* pp. 215, 219, 224.
31 *MB* p. 222.
32 *MB* p. 204.
33 *CN* Dec 1985.
34 *CN* April 1986.
35 *MB* p. 240.
36 *MB* p. 237.
37 *MB* p. 246.
38 *MB* pp. 253, 255.

Appendix One

The Bishops of Oxford

1542   Robert King, formerly Suffragan of Lincoln, first Bishop of Oxford, the seat of the Bishopric being at Osney

1559   Thomas Goldwell, Bishop of St Asaph; 1558 Fled to Milan and Rome

(See vacant nine years)

1567   Hugh Coren or Curwen, Archbishop of Dublin

(See vacant twenty-one years)

1589   John Underhill, Rector of Lincoln College

(See vacant eleven years)

1604   John Bridges, Dean of Salisbury

1619   John Howson, Student of Christ Church

1628   Richard Corbet, Dean of Christ Church

1632   *John Bancroft, Master of University College. Built Cuddesdon palace.[1]

1641   Robert Skinner, Bishop of Bristol (deprived during the Commonwealth, but restored 1660). Lived in Palace before its burning.

1663   William Paul, Dean of Lichfield

1665   Walter Blandford, Warden of Wadham College

1671   Nathanael, Lord Crewe, Rector of Lincoln College and Dean of Chichester

1674   Henry Compton, Canon of Christ Church

1676   John Fell, Dean of Christ Church. Rebuilt palace and returned to Cuddesdon.

1686   Samuel Parker, Archdeacon of Canterbury

1688   Timothy Hall (denied installation by the Chapter of Christ Church)

1690   John Hough, President of Magdalen College

1699   William Talbot, Dean of Worcester

1715   John Potter, Regius Professor of Divinity

1737   Thomas Secker, Bishop of Bristol

1758   John Hume, Bishop of Bristol
1766   *Robert Louth, Bishop of St David's (memorial in churchyard)
1777   John Butler, Prebendary of Winchester
1788   Edward Smallwell, Bishop of St David's
1799   John Randolph, Regius Professor of Divinity
1807   *Charles Moss (buried 23 Dec 1811 (aged 49))
1812   *William Jackson, Regius Professor of Greek (buried 16 Dec 1815, aged 65)
1816   Hon. Edward Legge, Dean of Windsor
1827   Charles Lloyd, Regius Professor of Divinity
1829   Richard Bagot, Dean of Canterbury
1845   Samuel Wilberforce, Dean of Westminster
1870   John Fielder Mackarness, Prebendary of Exeter
1889   *William Stubbs, Bishop of Chester
1901   Francis Paget, Dean of Christ Church
1911   Charles Gore, Bishop of Birmingham (resigned See of Oxford 1919)
1919   *Hubert Murray Burge, Bishop of Southwark
1925   Thomas Banks Strong, Bishop of Ripon (resigned See of Oxford 1937)
1937   Kenneth Escott Kirk, Regius Professor of Moral and Pastoral Theology. Did not reside in Cuddesdon.
1955   *Harry James Carpenter, Warden of Keble (resigned See of Oxford 1970). Returned to Cuddesdon in 1962. Ashes interred in Cuddesdon churchyard
1971   Kenneth John Woollcombe, Principal of Edinburgh Theological College (resigned See of Oxford 1978). Last bishop to live in Cuddesdon
1978   Patrick Campbell Rodger, Bishop of Manchester (resigned See of Oxford 1986)
1987   Richard Douglas Harries, Dean of King's College, London

* Asterisk denotes buried in church or churchyard.

Appendix Two

Cuddesdon Clergy

Rectors

(1189	Robert the Chaplain officiating)
Before 1206	Nicholas
c. 1206	John, Cardinal of SS. Cosman and Damian
c. 1216	John, Cardinal of St Praxed

15 December 1237: *Abingdon Abbey granted the rectory of Cuddesdon; a vicarage is endowed and the advowson granted to the abbey.*

Vicars and other clergy ministering in Cuddesdon parish (with date of institution if known)

1239	Richard (Vicar)
1247	Thomas de Haregrafe
1251	Johannes de Gnatteshal
1260	Ralph-The-Priest (?)
1270	Roger de Sutton
Before 1301	John
1307	Robert Putrel (dcn)
1310	William de Middleton (chapl)
1329	William Broyin (Vicar) (known as Brown)
1354	William de Henreth (exchanged living of St Mary's, Wallingford with Brown)
Before 1379	Richard Whaddon
1379	Henry Baker
Before 1410	John Salford
1412	William Messager (chapl)
Before 1435	Richard Plummer alias Whitewell (chapl)
1462	M. James Preston
1465	M. William Laughton
1466	M. Robert Lawles
1472	M. John Bulcombe

1473	M. William Axbryge
1481	M. John Lovier
1484	John Horetop
1494	M. John Edmund or Estmondi (Vicar)
1497	William Barrow (also Rector of Tackley)
1504	John Aspeden
1509	Thomas Chetwyn (mentioned in court case v. William Buk PRO C 1/288/76)
1514	Stephen Brawdribbe (pensioned Vicar in 1526)
1524	Richard Stoke (Vicar) d. 1546
1527	Robert Forylle and John Watt (Chaplains in Wheatley)

29 May 1537:   *Abingdon Abbey dissolved. Rectory reverts to the crown.*

1544	John Tyms (Curate)
2 Dec 1546	John Robyns (patronage exercised by John Broke, Clerk)
1558	Richard Clowdesley
3 Feb 1573/4-1606	Ralph Marler BD, Vicar, married in Cuddesdon 27 April 1579.
1577	William Meadcalfe (Curate) buried 27 August 1577.
1578/99	John Cooke (Curate)

1589:   *Advowson invested with the Bishop of Oxford and rectory granted as part of the endowment of diocese.*

30 Aug 1606	Edmund Underhill (Vicar), buried at Cuddesdon 5 October 1632. (Matriculated at Brasenose College, Oxford, 23 April 1586, BA Lincoln, 31 Oct 1590, MA 15 May 1594.)
1632	Bishop John Bancroft appointed himself Vicar *in commendam*

1637   *Vicarage of Cuddesdon appropriated by Bishop. 1637 to 1852: Bishops of Oxford were vicars of Cuddesdon*

1646	Bishop Skinner sequestrated from the vicarage and replaced by W. Beecher.
16 Nov 1648	Robert Easton

1660   *Bishops of Oxford resume occupation of vicarage*

Ministers/Curates (this list comprises all the ministers known to have served in Cuddesdon and Wheatley)

1668	Thomas Fulkes
c. 1670	Abraham Simmons
1685	C. Smith
1690	Daniel Slaymaker (or Sleamaker)
1705	J. Heyman (M)
1708	John Holland
1711	Thomas Clymer
1715	John Holland/Thomas Clymer
1721	J. Parsons
	John Rosse
1727	Joseph Gerrard
1734/39	William Walker
1735	John Wollin
1736	W. Haward
1737	Walter Ward
1738	Thomas Warneford
1740	Thomas Forster (to 1757)
1743	John Aynsley
1757	George Berkeley
1758	Henry Barton
1759	John Howell
1759	Arthur or Alexander Coham
1760	Mathew Spry
1764	John Vicary
1765	Daniel Peate
1768	John Lucas
1772	Herbert Randolph
1777	John Parkinson
1779	Henry Ford (to 1788)
1782	A. Deeve
1784	D. Stodartt or Hodatt
19 June 1788	Thomas Davies
1804	Edward Berins or Berens
1804	Richard Budd
1806	Thomas Percy
1807	John Ballard
1809	John Crosby Clark
1819	Henry Bishop; Richard Downs (Wheatley)

1824-35	W.H. Langdale (Wheatley)
1828	Augustus Page Saunders
1832	George A. Denison; left 1838
1839-45	A. Goldney, chaplain to Bishop Bagot; left to go to Bath and Wells
1845	William Thomson
1847	Alfred Pott
1851	Henry John Pye (1827-1903)
1852	Augustus Venables (Curate)
1853	George F. W. Igress (Curate)

Vicars

15 May 1852	*Vicarage separated from see by Act of Parliament*
3 June 1854	Alfred Pott inducted as Vicar and also becomes Principal of Theological College
15 Feb 1855	*Wheatley living established as a perpetual curacy*
6 May 1859	*Henry Hutchinson Swinny
1 March 1863	Edward King (res. 24 June 1873)
26 July 1873	*Charles Wellington Furse
23 July 1884	*William Methuen Gordon Ducat
15 April 1895	*John Octavius Johnston
28 Jan 1914	James Buchanan Seaton
Jan 1929	Eric Graham
3 Feb 1945	Kenneth Riches
25 Oct1952	Edward Knapp-Fisher
16 Sept 1960	Robert Runcie
17 July 1970	J. Leslie Houlden
25 Oct. 1977	David Wilcox (licensed initially as priest-in-charge. Collated as Vicar on 22 December 1982)
25 April 1986	John Garton

Team Vicars in the Wheatley Team Ministry

19 Sept 1996	Richard Cowles

Bibliography

A. Unpublished Papers

1. Parish Archives
PCC Minute Books, 1917-38; 1970-88
Applications for faculties and archdeacon's certificates
Handwritten copy of registers to end of eighteenth century
Anonymous handwritten history and exercise book of notes on the church
Script to 'A Distant View' by Maida Stainer
Insurance Valuation, June 1978
Programme for visit of Archbishop of Canterbury, 1-2 November 1980
All Saints' Church, Cuddesdon, Organ Appeal

2. Bodleian Library, Oxford:
Oxford Archdeacon's Court records (MS Top Oxon c. 103)
Visitors' book of bishop's palace (MS Wilberforce e. 16)
Notebooks containing notes on fabric and furniture (MS Top Oxon e. 565)
Letter E. T. Leeds to Dr A. W. Coombs (Bod. MS Top. Oxon d. 188).
Andrew Atherstone, 'Charles Golightly (1807-1885), Church Parties and
    University Politics in Victorian Oxford', Oxford D. Phil. thesis, 2000
S. S. Pearce, *The Clergy of the Deanery of Cuddesdon*, handlist.
Proposals for the Restoration of Cuddesdon Church (handbill) (Bod. G.A. Oxon c.
    317 (7))
All Saints Church Cuddesdon Choir Rules (Bod. G.A. Oxon c. 317 (7))
Various Pictures of Cuddesdon.

3. Oxfordshire County Record Office:
Cuddesdon Parish Records: MSS D.D. Par Cuddesdon (CPR): A: Registers
    from 1541 to date; B: Vestry Minutes 1821-1928; C: Churchwarden's and
    Offertory Accounts, 1705-1945; D: Constables Accounts, 1735-1835; E:
    Poor Rate Book; F: Registers of Services 1910-60; G: Other Papers.
Oxford Archdeaconry Records
Oxford Diocesan Papers (ODP): Bishop's visitation returns for most years;
    Bishop Fell's Book; Faculty applications (c. 1788 uncatalogued).

4. *Centre for Oxfordshire Studies*
Various Photographs of Cuddesdon; newspaper cuttings.

5. *Ripon College Cuddesdon*
Various Photographs of Cuddesdon and papers relating to the College.

B. Published Sources

1. Journals and Newspapers

All Saints Church, Cuddesdon News. January 1959 to February 1973.
Antiquaries Journal
Archaeological Journal
The Berks, Bucks and Oxon Archaeological Journal
Church Times
Cuddesdon News, from March 1973.
The Guardian
Illustrated London News
Journal of Roman Studies
Medieval Archaeology
Oxford Architectural Society
Oxford Architectural Society Meeting
Oxford Mail
Oxford Times
Oxford Times Limited Edition Magazine
Oxfordshire Life
Proceedings of the Society of Antiquaries
Reading Mercury
The Rock
Thame Gazette
Oxoniensia
Proceedings of the Birmingham Philosophical Society

2. Books and Articles

2.1. Primary Sources

Anglo-Saxon Chronicle (Everyman edition), London: Dent, 1953
Margaret Archer (ed.), *Register of Bp. Philip Repingdon, 1405-1419*, i, LRS 57
(1962)
T. Astle, S. Ayscough and J. Caley (eds), *Taxatio Ecclesiastica Angliae et Walliae
auctoritate p. Nicholai IV, circa A.D. 1291* (19 Edward I), London: Record
Commission, 1802
Bede, *Ecclesiastical History*, ed. J. A. Giles, London: Bell, 1894.
Walter de Gray Birch, *Cartularium Saxonicum*, London: Whiting, 1885-1893

W. H. Bliss et al (eds), *Calendar of entries in the Papal Registers relating to Great Britain and Ireland (1198-1409)*, 4 vols, London: HMSO, 1893-1902

John R. Bloxham (ed.), *The Register of St Mary Magdalen's College*, Oxford, Oxford: Graham, 1853

Margaret Bowker (ed.), *An Episcopal Court Book for the Diocese of Lincoln: 1514-1520*, LRS 61, 1967

J. S. Brewer (ed), *Letters and Papers of Henry VIII*, London: HMSO, vol. iv (1), 1870

J. S. Brewer (ed), *Letters and Papers of Henry VIII*, London: HMSO, vol. xii (1), 1890

E. R. Brinkworth (ed.), *The Archdeacon's court: Liber actorum, 1584*, ORS 23, 1942

The Bishop's House, Cuddesdon (Sale catalogue for auction held 26th September 1978), Oxford: E.J. Brooks, 1978.

C. R. and M. G. Cheney (eds.), *Letters of Innocent III, 1198-1216 concerning England and Wales*, Oxford: Clarendon, 1967

Nehemiah Curnock (ed.), *The Journal of the Rev. John Wesley AM*, London: Epworth, 1938

F. N. Davis (ed.), *Rotuli Roberti Grosseteste*, London: Canterbury and York Society, 10, 1913

F. N. Davis (ed.), *Rotuli Roberti Grosseteste and Henry of Lexington*, LRS 11, 1914

F. N. Davis (ed.), *Rotuli Ricardi Gravesend*, LRS 20, 1925

F. N. Davis (ed.), *Parochial Collections made by Anthony à Wood, MA and Richard Rawlinson*, ORS 2, 1920

William Dugdale, *Monasticon Anglicanum*, London: Longman, 1817

Konrad Eubel, *Hierarchia Catholica medii aevi,* Monasterii: Sumptibus et typis Librariae Regensbergianae, 1898-1910.

Kenneth Fincham (ed.) *Visitation Articles and Injunctions of the Early Stuart Church*, Woodbridge: Boydell and Brewer (Church of England Record Society 5), vol. 2, 1994

Anne P. Fuller (ed.), *Calendar of Papal Registers Relating to Great Britain and Ireland*, Dublin: Irish Stationery Office, vol. 16, 1986

James Gairdner and R.H. Brodie (eds.), *Letters and Papers of Henry VIII*, London: HMSO, vol. xiv (1), 1894

G. N. Garmonsway (ed.), *Anglo-Saxon Chronicle* (Everyman edition), London: Dent, 1953. Rose Graham (ed.), *The Edwardian Inventories for Oxfordshire*, ORS 1, 1919

G. B. Grundy (ed. and tr.), *Saxon Oxfordshire: Charters and Ancient Highways*, ORS 15, 1933

W. O. Hassall (ed.), *Wheatley Records, 956-1056*, ORS, 36, 1956

John Hudson (ed.), *Historia Ecclesie Abbendonensis: The History of the Church in Abingdon*, vol. ii, Oxford: Clarendon Press, 2002 (*HEA*)

A. P. Jenkins (ed.), *The Correspondence of Thomas Secker*, ORS 57, 1991

H. A. Lloyd Jukes (ed.), *Articles of Enquiry Addressed to the Clergy of the Diocese of Oxford at the Primary Visitation of Dr. Thomas Secker*, 1738, ORS 38, 1957

S. E. Kelly (ed.), *Anglo-Saxon Charters*, Oxford: Clarendon Press, 2000

R. E. G. Kirk (ed.), *Accounts of the Obedientiars of Abingdon Abbey*, London: Camden Society, 1891-2

Agnes M. Leys (ed.), *The Sandford Cartulary*, ORS 19, 1938

William E. Lunt (ed.), *Valuation of Norwich*, Oxford: Clarendon Press, 1926

William Dunn Macray, *A Register of the Members of St Mary Magdalen College, Oxford*, London: Froude, vol. 1, 1894

John Morris (ed.) *Domesday Book: Parallel Latin text and English Translation*, vol. 14: Oxfordshire, Chichester: Phillimore, 1978

Nonarum inquisitiones in Curia scaccarii: temp. regis Edwardi iii, London: Record Commission, 1807

Francis Palgrave (ed.), *Nomina Villarum*, (Parliamentary Writs, Writs of Military Summons), London: Public Records Commission, 1834

R. K. Pugh (ed.), *The Letter-Books of Samuel Wilberforce* ORS 47, 1970.

H. E. Salter (ed.), *A Subsidy Collected in the Diocese of Lincoln in 1526*, ORS 63 (1909)

H. E. Salter (ed.), *Oseney Abbey Cartulary*, iv, Oxford: Oxford Historical Society, 97, 1934

H. E. Salter (ed.), *Snappe's formulary and other records*, Oxford: Oxford Historical Society, 80, 1924

C.F. Slade and Gabrielle Lambrick (eds.), *Two Cartularies of Abingdon Abbey*, vol. 1: Lyell Cartulary (*LC*); vol. 2: Chatsworth Cartulary (*CC*), Oxford: OHS, 1990.

David Smith (ed.), *English Episcopal Acta (Lincoln)*, Oxford: Oxford University Press, vol. 4, 1986

Joseph Stevenson (ed.), *Chronicon Monasterii de Abingdon*, Rolls Series, 2 vols, vol. i, *From the Foundation of the Monastery Until the Norman Conquest*; vol. ii, *From the Conquest until the accession of Richard I*, London: Longman, 1858 (*CMA*)

A. Hamilton Thompson (ed.), *Visitations in the Diocese of Lincoln*, 1517-31, LRS vols 33, 35, 37, 1940-7

Kate Tiller (ed.), *Church and Chapel in Oxfordshire*, ORS 55, 1987

Vita Sancti Birini in Rosalind C. Love (ed.), *Three Eleventh-Century Anglo-Latin Saints' Lives*, Oxford: Oxford University Press (Oxford Medieval Texts), 1996, pp. 1-47

S. R. Wigram (ed.), *The Cartulary of the Monastery of St. Frideswide at Oxford*, OHS, 28, 31, 1895-96 (*SFC*)

2.2. Secondary Sources

J. Y. Akerman, *Remains of Pagan Saxondom*, London: John Russell, 1855

W. J. Andrew and R. A. Smith, 'The Winchester Anglo-Saxon Bowl' in

Antiquaries Journal 11 (1931)

Harold Anson, *T.B. Strong*, London: SPCK, 1949

A. R. Ashwell, *Life of Bishop Wilberforce*, 3 vols, London: John Murray, 1880

Frank Barlow, *The English Church 1000-1066: A Constitutional History*, London: Longmans, 1963

Frank Barlow, *The English Church, 1066-1154*, London: Longmans, 1979

G. F. A. Best, *Temporal Pillars*, Cambridge: Cambridge University Press, 1964

M. Biddle, Gabrielle Lambrick, J. N. L. Myers, 'The Early History of Abingdon, Berkshire, and its Abbey' in *Medieval Archaeology* 12 (1968) pp. 26-69.

John Blair, *Anglo-Saxon Oxfordshire*, Stroud and Oxford: Alan Sutton (Oxfordshire Books), 1994

C. J. Bond, 'The Reconstruction of a Medieval Landscape: the Estates of Abingdon Abbey' in *Landscape History* 1 (1979), pp. 59-75

Margaret Bowker, *The Secular Clergy in the Diocese of Lincoln, 1495-1520*, Cambridge: Cambridge University Press, 1968

Margaret Bowker, *The Henrician Reformation in the Diocese of Lincoln under John Longland, 1521-1547*, Cambridge: Cambridge University Press, 1981

Grace Briggs, Jean Cook and Trevor Rowley (eds), *The Archaeology of the Oxford Region*, Oxford: Oxford University Department for External Studies, 1986

G. Baldwin Brown, *The Arts in Early England*, London: John Murray, 7 vols, 1903-37

Humphrey Carpenter, *Robert Runcie. The Reluctant Archbishop*, London: Hodder and Stoughton, 1996

Owen Chadwick, *The Founding of Cuddesdon*, Oxford: Oxford University Press, 1954

Owen Chadwick, *Michael Ramsey. A life*, Oxford: Oxford University Press, 1991

Mark D. Chapman (ed.), *Ambassadors of Christ*, Aldershot: Ashgate, 2004

Lord Charnwood (ed.), *Discourses and Letters of Hubert Murray Burge*, London: Chatto and Windus, 1930

C. R. Cheney, *From Becket to Langton*, Manchester: Manchester University Press, 1956

J. C. Cole, 'The Building of the Second Palace at Cuddesdon' in *Oxoniensia* 24-5 (1959-60), pp. 49-69

Martin Conway, 'Burgundian Buckles and Coptic Influences' in *Proceedings of the Society of Antiquaries* 30 (1918), pp. 63-89

Joyce Coombs, *George Anthony Denison. The Firebrand*, London: Faith Press, 1984

Emma Cownie, *Religious Patronage in Anglo-Norman England, 1066-1135*, Woodbridge: Boydell for the Royal Historical Society, 1998

Mieneke Cox *The Story of Abingdon*, Abingdon: Mieneke Cox, 1989

Thomas Cox, *A Topographical, Ecclesiastical and Natural History of Oxfordshire*, Savoy, 1700

Cuddesdon College, Record and Memorial, Oxford: Oxford University Press, 1904

Cuddesdon College. A Record and Memorial, Oxford: Oxford University Press, 1929

E. A. Davies, *Cuddesdon. Its Story*, Cuddesdon (privately published), 1950

George Anthony Denison, *Notes on My Life, 1805-1878*, London: James Parker, 1878

Tania M. Dickinson, *Cuddesdon and Dorchester-on-Thames, Oxfordshire: two early Saxon princely sites in Wessex*, Oxford: British Archaeological Reports, 1974

D. C. Douglas, 'Some early surveys from the Abbey of Abingdon' in *English Historical Review* 44 (1929), pp. 618-25

W. M. G. Ducat, *The Story of Cuddesdon Parish Church. A Sermon*, Preached in the Parish Church, 13 November 1887, (privately printed), Oxford, 1887

Margaret Duggan, *Runcie. The Making of an Archbishop*, London: Hodder and Stoughton, 1983

David Eddershaw, *The Civil War in Oxfordshire*, Stroud: Alan Sutton, 1995

Lord Elton, *Edward King and Our Times*, London: Geoffrey Bles, 1958

Frank Emery, *The Making of the Oxfordshire Landscape*, London: Hodder and Stoughton, 1974

J. E. Field, *Saint Berin. The Apostle of Wessex*, London: SPCK, 1902

John Fox, *The Reformation in the Villages*, Wheatley: Privately Printed, 1996

John Fox, *Tanning-Barn to Church. The Dissenting Congregation of Wheatley over Two Hundred Years*, Wheatley URC, 1997

John Fox (ed.), *One More Millennium: The Story of Wheatley and Holton Park*, Wheatley: Wheatley 2000, 2000

C. W. Furse, *The Beauty of Holiness: Meditations and Addresses*, London: John Murray, 1903

Michael Furse, *Stand Therefore! A Bishop's Testimony of Faith in the Church of England*, London: SPCK, 1953

Margaret Gallyon, *The Early Church in Wessex and Mercia*, Lavenham: Dalton, 1980

Margaret Gelling, *The Placenames of Oxfordshire*, (2 vols) Cambridge: Cambridge University Press, 1953-4, English Place Names Society (*EPNS*), vols 23, 24

William Ewart Gladstone, *A Chapter of Autobiography*, London: John Murray, 1868

C. P. Golightly, *A Solemn Warning against Cuddesdon College*, Oxford (privately printed), 1878

R. T. Günther, *The Oxford Country*, London: John Murray, 1912

Helena Hamrow, 'Anglo-Saxon Oxfordshire, 400-700' in *Oxoniensia* 64 (1999)

W. O. Hassall, 'The History of Cuddesdon' in *Thame Gazette*, 20 February 1951

Sonia Chadwick Hawkes, 'The Early Saxon Period' in Grace Briggs, Jean Cook and Trevor Rowley (eds), *The Archaeology of the Oxford Region*, Oxford: Oxford University Department for External Studies, 1986, pp. 64-108

Christopher Hill, *Economic Problems of the Church from Whitgift to the Long Parliament*, Oxford: Clarendon Press, 1956

Henry Scott Holland, *Creed and Character*, London: Longmans, 1887

Henry Scott Holland, *A Bundle of Memories*, London: Wells Gardner, Darton & Co., 1915

Robert T. Holtby, *Eric Graham*, London: Oxford University Press, 1967

W. H. Hutton, *Letters of William Stubbs, Bishop of Oxford*, London: Constable, 1904

Mary Jessup, *A History of Oxfordshire*, London: Phillimore, 1975

Eric John, *Land Tenure in Early England*, Leicester: Leicester University Press, London, 1960.

John Kemble, *Codex Diplomaticus aevi saxonici*, Londini: Sumptibus Societatis, 1839-1848

Eric Kemp, *Kenneth Kirk, Bishop of Oxford, 1937-54*, London: Hodder, 1959

J. Kenward, 'A first note on the Anglo-Saxon Cemetery at Wheatley, Oxon' in *Proceedings of the Birmingham Philosophical Society* 4 (1884), p. 179

H. Kirk-Smith, *William Thomson, Archbishop of York: His Life and Times, 1819-90*, London: SPCK, 1958

Gabrielle Lambrick, 'Abingdon Abbey Administration' in *Journal of Ecclesiastical History* 17 (1966), pp. 159-183

E. T. Leeds, 'An Anglo-Saxon Cemetery at Wheatley' in *Proceedings of the Society of Antiquaries* 29 (1916-17), pp. 48-65

Rosalind C. Love (ed.), *Three Eleventh-Century Anglo-Latin Saints' Lives*, Oxford: Oxford University Press (Oxford Medieval Texts), 1996

Charles Coleridge Mackarness, *Memorials of the Episcopate of John Fielder Mackarness, D.D., Bishop of Oxford*, Oxford: Parker, 1892

Edward Marshall, *Diocesan Histories: Oxford*, London: SPCK, 1882

Henry Mayr-Harting, *The Coming of Christianity to Anglo-Saxon England*, London: Batsford, 1972

Standish Meacham, *Lord Bishop*, Cambridge MA: Harvard University Press, 1970

John A. Newton, *Search for a Saint: Edward King*, London: Epworth, 1977

Malcom Oxley, 'Wheatley in the Valley. Cuddesdon on the Hill' in Blair Worden, *Stuart England*, London: Phaidon, 1986

Stephen Paget (ed.), *Henry Scott Holland. Memoir and Letters*, London: John Murray, 1921

Stephen Paget and J.M.C. Crum, *Life of Francis Paget*, London: Macmillan, 1912

W. A. Pantin, 'The Oxford Architectural and Historical Society' in *Oxoniensia*, 4 (1939), pp. 174-94

J. H. Parker, *A Guide to the Architectural Antiquities in the Neighbourhood of Oxford*, Deanery of Cuddesdon, Oxford: John Henry Parker, 1846

Nikolaus Pevsner and Jennifer Sherwood, *The Buildings of England: Oxfordshire,*

Harmondsworth: Penguin, 1974

N. J. G. Pounds, *A History of the English Parish*, Cambridge: Cambridge University Press, 2000

Alfred Pott, *Village Sermons*, London: Bell and Daldy, 1867

Alfred Pott, *Confirmation Lectures delivered to a Village Congregation in the Diocese of Oxford*, London: Masters, 1852

G. L. Prestige, *Life of Charles Gore*, London: Heinemann, 1935

B. W. Randolph and J. W. Townroe, *The Mind and Work of Bishop King*, London: Mowbray, 1918

G. W. E. Russell, *Edward King*, London: Smith, Elder, 1912

Frederick Sharpe, *The Church Bells of Oxfordshire*, ORS 28, 1949

R. H. Snape, *English Monastic Finances in the Later Middle Ages*, Cambridge: Cambridge University Press, 1926

John Steane, *Oxfordshire*, London: Pimlico County History Guide, 1996.

F. M. Stenton, *The Early History of the Abbey of Abingdon*, Stamford: Paul Watkins, (reprint), 1989

William Stubbs, *A Charge delivered to the Clergy and Churchwardens of the Diocese*, Oxford: Oxford University Press, June 1890

Peter Summers (ed.), *Hatchments of Britain*, London: Phillimore, 1974-94

Alan Thacker, 'Aethelwold and Abingdon' in Yorke (ed.), *Bishop Aethelwold*, pp. 43-64

Hilary L. Turner, *Oxfordshire. A Look at the Past*, Derby: Plotwood Press, 1997

Samuel Wilberforce, *Sermons Preached on Various Occasions*, Oxford: Parker, 1877

A Browne Willis, *A Survey of the Cathedrals*, London: R. Gosling, 1730

Anthony à Wood, *Athenae Oxonienses*, (ed. P. Bliss), London: Rivington, 1815

A. Clark (ed.), *The Life and Times of Anthony Wood, antiquary of Oxford, 1632-1695*, OHS 26, vol. 2, 1892

Blair Worden, *Stuart England*, London: Phaidon, 1986

Barbara Yorke (ed.), *Bishop Aethelwold: His Career and Influence*, Woodbridge: Boydell, 1988

Barbara Yorke, *Kings and Kingdoms of Early Anglo-Saxon England*, London: Routledge, 1997

Index

(Abbots of Abingdon, Vicars, Rectors and Curates of Cuddesdon, and Bishops of Oxford, are noted in brackets)